W9-AWA-045

22

Shooting Star

TOM WICKER

Shooting Star

THE BRIEF ARC OF JOE MCCARTHY

★ ★ ★

Harcourt, Inc.

Orlando   Austin   New York   San Diego   Toronto   London

Requests for permission to make copies of any part
of the work should be mailed to the following address:
Permissions Department, Harcourt, Inc.,
6277 Sea Harbor Drive, Orlando, Florida 32887-6777.

www.HarcourtBooks.com

Library of Congress Cataloging-in-Publication Data
Wicker, Tom.
Shooting star: the brief arc of Joe McCarthy/
Tom Wicker.—1st ed.
p.   cm.
Includes bibliographical references and index.
1. McCarthy, Joseph, 1908–1957.   2. Legislators—United
States—Biography.   3. United States. Congress. Senate—
Biography.   4. Anti-communist movements—United
States—History—20th century.   5. Internal security—
United States—History—20th century.   6. United States—
Politics and government—1945–1953.   7. United States—
Politics and government—1953–1961.   I. Title.
E748.M143W53   2006
973.921'092—dc22   2005020990
ISBN-13: 978-0-15-101082-0   ISBN-10: 0-15-101082-X

Text set in Fairfield
Designed by Lydia D'moch

Printed in the United States of America

First edition
A C E G I K J H F D B

For Kathleen C. Wicker . . . and the parents who guided us

"A very complicated character."
—*Robert F. Kennedy*

Shooting Star

Prologue

ONE JANUARY MORNING in Washington in 1957, as I walked along a marble-and-tile corridor of the Old Senate Office Building, only the sound of my footfalls broke the silence. Along either side of the corridor, tall official doors guarded senators' offices; and one other person was visible, a man coming toward me from too far away for me to see his face.

That day I had started work as the first resident Washington correspondent for the *Winston-Salem (NC) Journal*. One of the trolley cars that in the 1950s still plied Washington's streets took me along Pennsylvania Avenue to the Capitol, and I had walked across its great plaza to what is now called the Russell Office Building. An elevator took me to my floor, and I emerged into that immensely long corridor stretching the length of a city block—the man at the other end a small dark figure in the distance.

He and I were a long time moving together in what seemed like a tunnel lined by those imposing office doors. As we neared one another, I became gratefully aware that his heels, too, were clacking on the hard corridor floor. But no other sound broke the cold marble silence of the Senate Office Building. The approaching man seemed to stagger slightly just as I sensed something familiar about him, as if he were someone I might have once known.

Nevertheless, I felt myself to be an intruder and I decided to pass without a word. But when we were a few feet apart, the other man stopped, grinned broadly, and thrust out his hand. I had no choice but to take it. His hand shook and was clammy despite a vigorous grip; a day's stubble tinged his square jaw, gone a little flabby; and the unmistakable odor of whiskey clung to him in the corridor air.

"Glad to see you, sir! Always glad to see real Amer'cans here'n these fancy halls!"

I realized immediately that I was a voter being given a politician's glad hand. I was not so quick to see that this shabby person was the infamous Joseph R. McCarthy of Wisconsin, once the scourge of communism, the menacing enforcer of real Americanism, the feared senator who had not quailed even before President Eisenhower. But how could that be?

McCarthy's anticommunist campaign had long been discredited. He had been condemned by the Senate. For years Eisenhower had officially ignored him. He had reportedly become an excessive drinker. But this sour-smelling creature so eager to shake my hand? *The* Joe McCarthy?

"'S'your building, y'know," he insisted. "More'n any of"—
he made a dismissing gesture toward the forbidding office
doors—"these big shots. It's your place, sir!"

I was discomfited to come face-to-face with a man
whom—at long range but for years—I had held in contempt.
But his wide grin, his shaky but hearty grip, his unconcealed
eagerness were somehow intriguing. He pumped my hand
again, asking, "Anything I can do for you?"—as if he really
wanted to know.

I found myself smiling, too, even returning the handshake—but then I remembered who he was, dropped his
hand, brushed past, and hurried down the corridor. I might
have reacted differently had my mind not been so filled with
bitter preconceptions. Or maybe not. I was young, and youth
has little taste for generosity.

Later I learned that an important part of Joe McCarthy's
personal and political appeal in Wisconsin had been his willingness to approach perfect strangers, pump their hands or
throw his arm around their shoulders, and proclaim his need,
even his hunger, for their votes and their affection. In his
early years, he had been notoriously able to read and respond
to others' feelings—as he seemed to intuit my sense of being
out of place in the Old Senate Office Building.

More than forty years after this chance meeting, when the
senator was long dead, my work on a book about Dwight
Eisenhower left me oddly impressed by McCarthy's audacity,
amounting often to recklessness, and his headlong engagements

with his opponents (even with the revered "father figure" in the White House). I was impressed, too, by what had been his obvious hunger—for power, surely, but perhaps for regard as well. He had taken on practically all comers, outsmarted and outmaneuvered most, laughing sometimes at their frustration, occasionally consoling them, surviving usually for another fight—as if fighting itself, particularly against the odds, made life worth living for Joe McCarthy.

A half century ago, in that chill marble hall, impressions from my own past were powerfully present, and I was unable to see beyond the shadow I had encountered. I did not know then that I had glimpsed not only what was left of Joe McCarthy—but also what power comes to, perhaps what we all come to.

1

No wonder I moved on so promptly in 1957. Joe McCarthy may have been the most destructive demagogue in American history. As a small-town reporter obsessed with national affairs, I was certain during the years of McCarthy's political dominance that he was uniquely villainous, his sins against democracy not to be forgiven or forgotten.

However interminable those years seemed to me, they were in fact relatively few. Joe McCarthy first became visible to the nation on February 9, 1950, when he delivered a Lincoln Day address to local Republicans in Wheeling, West Virginia. That night, according to various and differing accounts, he declared something like "I have here in my hand a list of 205" members of the Communist Party, "still working and shaping policy in the State Department."

Just less than five years after that speech, following December 2, 1954, McCarthy virtually disappeared. That day the

United States Senate—his power base, his political bunker—voted by sixty-seven to twenty-two to "condemn" him for conduct bringing that body into disrepute. Every Democratic senator except John F. Kennedy of Massachusetts, who was in the hospital, voted for what most senators believed to be a resolution of "censure."* Twenty-two Republicans—members of the party that had done the most to advance and sustain McCarthy—joined the Democrats, some with relief at the end of a political reign they had considered an ordeal.

Even this climactic moment of defeat brought out McCarthy's peculiar jauntiness:

"It wasn't," he told the reporters who had done so much to spread his fame and power, "exactly a vote of confidence."

He then added with characteristic bravado and exaggeration:

"I'm happy to have this circus over, so I can get back to the real work of digging out communism, corruption, and crime."

He never did. Strictly speaking, he never had.

McCARTHY'S WHEELING SPEECH in February 1950 is one of the most consequential in U.S. history without a recorded or an agreed-upon text, nor was it connected to a noteworthy cause such as an inaugural or a commemoration; instead, it resulted from ordinary political bureaucracy. The Republican

---

* *Webster's* makes little distinction between "condemn" and "censure." "Censure" does not appear, however, in the text of the resolution, though it was originally in the title.

Party's speaker's bureau had routinely assigned McCarthy, then a little-known one-term senator regarded unfavorably by many of his colleagues, to a five-speech Lincoln Day tour that began in Wheeling and ended in Huron, South Dakota— hardly major political forums. Party elders had no idea what he would say, other than the usual political balderdash; neither, probably, did McCarthy, who arrived in Wheeling with two rough drafts—one concerning housing, then his Senate "specialty," the other on communists in government.

The origins of the second speech are undetermined but not totally obscure. As early as his winning Senate campaign against Democrat Howard McMurray in 1946,* McCarthy had used "Red scare" rhetoric, enough so that McMurray complained in one of the campaign debates that his loyalty had never before been challenged by a "responsible citizen . . . [T]his statement is a little below the belt." That did not deter McCarthy from repeating the accusation and others like it.[1]

In later years McCarthy gave different reasons for his ultimate turn, after four relatively undistinguished years in the Senate, to all-out Red hunting. On various occasions McCarthy cited a warning from Secretary of the Navy James Forrestal about the dangers of communist infiltration; an investigation of fur imports that uncovered the Soviet Union's

---

* McCarthy had assured himself of a Senate nomination by defeating the incumbent, Robert M. La Follette Jr., in an earlier Republican primary.

use of its fur trade to advance its espionage; an invitation from an unspecified FBI team to take on the communist problem; the defeat of Leland Olds for reappointment as chairman of the Federal Power Commission after hearings in which senators led by Lyndon B. Johnson decided that Olds was maybe a Red or anyway at least too radical; and the exposure of Alger Hiss and his conviction for perjury on January 21, 1950, just before the Wheeling speech.

None of these events is convincing as a real turning point. Forrestal, for example, was dead when McCarthy's claim appeared, so that it could not be checked with him, and the fur-import yarn is implausible on its face. More believable is a story first published by the late columnist Drew Pearson about a dinner in January 1950 at Washington's once-popular, now-defunct Colony Restaurant. That night, Pearson reported, McCarthy entertained Father Edmund Walsh, dean of the Georgetown University School of Foreign Service; William A. Roberts, a Washington attorney who represented Pearson; and Charles Kraus, a fervently anticommunist speechwriter for McCarthy. The senator sought advice, Pearson wrote, on building a record for his reelection campaign in 1952; Father Walsh suggested "communism as an issue," and McCarthy supposedly leaped at the idea.

This tale has been widely accepted, but it, too, should be taken with a dash of skepticism. In the first place, "communism as an issue" had been a Republican staple for years.

(The Republican vice-presidential candidate in 1944, Senator John W. Bricker of Ohio, had tried even that early on to make the point: "First the New Deal took over the Democratic party and destroyed its very foundation; now these communist forces have taken over the New Deal and will destroy the very foundations of the Republic.") Red-baiting was a Republican tactic in which a leader as respected as Robert A. Taft of Ohio sometimes indulged. In the second place, a senator who had used alleged communism against Howard McMurray in 1946 and who was well aware of communism as a national political issue could hardly have been knocked off his horse, like Saul on the road to Damascus, by a suggestion that he retake a well-trodden path.

Even before the Colony dinner, McCarthy had blasted Secretary of State Dean Acheson for refusing "to turn his back" on Alger Hiss. In November 1949, moreover, McCarthy had furiously attacked one of his most bitter home-state enemies, the *Madison Capital Times,* in an eleven-page mimeographed statement claiming that the newspaper followed the communist line, aping the *Daily Worker* in its news treatment; that its city editor was known to its publisher as a communist; and that the *Capital Times*' anti-McCarthy investigations were communist inspired. McCarthy raised the question whether the *Capital Times* might be "the Red mouthpiece for the Communist party in Wisconsin?" He also called for an economic boycott of the paper (an action that never materialized). The statement was franked and mailed throughout Wisconsin.

The author of such an attack needed no suggestion from Father Walsh (who later repudiated McCarthy's extreme brand of anticommunism) to realize that "communism as an issue" was headline stuff. The assault on the *Capital Times** had already brought McCarthy more publicity in Wisconsin than any of his activities in the Senate.

McCarthy's Wheeling speech, far from being a sudden inspiration, reflected the senator's late debut in what by 1950 had become a full-dress Republican campaign against the communists, "fellow travelers, Reds, and pinks" that party spokesmen insisted (with good reason) had infiltrated (to an extent they exaggerated) the Democratic Party and the Roosevelt and Truman administrations. As far as has been verified over the years, McCarthy had nothing new or original to add to the campaign—save, crucially, the drama, hyperbole, and audacity of which he quickly showed himself a master.

In the rough draft McCarthy handed on February 9 to Wheeling reporters (who, at his jovial request, had counseled him to make the anticommunist rather than the housing speech), he openly plagiarized a newly famous predecessor in the Red-hunting field, Representative Richard M. Nixon of California:

---

* As was often to be the case later, no one seriously checked on the authenticity of McCarthy's charges.

NIXON (*to the House of Representatives, January 26, 1950*): The great lesson which should be learned from the Alger Hiss case is that we are not just dealing with espionage agents who get 30 pieces of silver to obtain the blueprints of a new weapon . . . but this is a far more sinister type of activity, because it permits the enemy to guide and shape our policy.

McCARTHY (*in the rough draft of his Wheeling speech on February 9, 1950*): One thing to remember in discussing the Communists in our government is that we are not dealing with spies who get 30 pieces of silver to steal the blueprint of a new weapon. We are dealing with a far more sinister type of activity because it permits the enemy to guide and shape our policy.

The senator also included a three-paragraph article written by the *Chicago Tribune's* Willard Edwards, a journalistic pioneer in anticommunist "investigations." Not only was anticommunism old stuff; Joe McCarthy was parroting a line frequently laid down by Nixon, reporters such as Edwards and George Sokolsky, the House Un-American Activities Committee (HUAC), numerous Republican oligarchs, and even some conservative Democrats (notably, Pat McCarran of Nevada).

The "real news" at Wheeling, if any, was in the specificity of McCarthy's numbers, as they were widely reported, and in the drama of his presentation—"I hold here in my hand" an incriminating document, *evidence*—after all the generalized perfidy his party had assigned to the Democrats and their New Deal and Fair Deal. At the outset Joe McCarthy displayed his gift for drama. He surely recognized then, too, the ease with which distortion, confidently expressed, could be made to seem fact.

McCARTHY WAS A LITTLE vague about the number that gave his speech much of its notoriety. Was it "205 . . . members of the Communist Party" in the State Department, as written by reporters who followed his rough draft as the speech was delivered? Or was it only 205 "bad risks" plus 57 "card-carrying communists," as McCarthy recalled the next day in Salt Lake City? Or was it just the 57 he claimed in Reno the day after that?

None of these numbers had any immediate provenance, other than their apparent factuality in the hands of a U.S. senator willing to use them. McCarthy in Wheeling seems to have been reading from or referring to a four-year-old letter written by former secretary of state James F. Byrnes to members of Congress[2]—not at all a secret document, since it had been printed in the *Congressional Record*. Byrnes had reported in 1946 that after the screening of 3,000 federal wartime employees being transferred to the State Department at the end of World War II, recommendations had been lodged against permanent employment for 285 of them. Of these, 71 had been discharged in 1946, which left 206—near enough to 205 for the offhand, clipped-together speech Mc-Carthy had made to Wheeling Republicans.[3]

What number McCarthy cited at Wheeling could not be precisely determined because a local radio operator had accidentally erased the tape of the speech. This would not have happened to Nixon, already basking in the public victory of Alger Hiss's perjury conviction. But the excitement and the headlines generated* by McCarthy's charges—whatever they were—as well as his repetitions, obfuscations, and contradictions in Colorado and Nevada, caused the story to be repeated and expanded into a national sensation.

When McCarthy's plane landed for a stopover in Denver the day after the Wheeling speech, for instance, he was besieged on the tarmac by local reporters. The *Denver Post* had played the AP story about the speech on its front page, and the press wanted to see the supporting documents. With his gift for mining favorable publicity out of adversity, McCarthy added suspense to the story by claiming to have misplaced the list of 205 or perhaps 57 names but promising to produce it later. An expanded story from Denver sped along his new fame. Sellout on high! And more to come! A U.S. senator had made an accusation that he claimed to be able to produce evidence for, that communists had infiltrated the State

---

* The *New York Times* and other major dailies ignored or knew nothing of McCarthy's speech, but the Associated Press carried an account across the country.

Department and were shaping its policy—hence, by implication, that of the Truman administration in the Cold War with the Soviet Union.

In February 1950 there were headline reasons why an imprecise speech delivered far from the mainstream by a virtually unknown senator with no expertise could excite a large part of the American people. Across the nation in late 1949 and early 1950, news columns and broadcasts were full of the Soviets' unexpected explosion of an atomic bomb, the arrests of eleven American communists for violations of the Smith Act, Hiss's perjury conviction, the arrest of Dr. Klaus Fuchs for atomic spying in Britain, and President Truman's announcement that work would begin on "the super"—the hydrogen bomb. McCarthy's charge seemed plausible after these revelations of internal subversion in a Cold War growing more and more dangerous.

The tidal wave of publicity and power that descended on Joe McCarthy after the Wheeling speech apparently flustered even him—witness his lack of preparation for the clamoring reporters he had not expected to meet him at the Denver airport. When making his charge, he had, most likely, only been seeking to serve his party by energizing and entertaining the good Republicans of West Virginia. Like a real tidal wave, however, the political roller that resulted was not without causes both obvious and obscure. It had only been waiting to happen.

———

Substantially, the times were responsible.

The United States had triumphed in World War II, defeating—almost single-handedly, as many Americans saw it—both the Nazis and the Japanese. But even before the troops came home, the most dangerous and persistent enemy turned out to be the wartime ally upon which Americans' wartime—Democratic—government had lavished support and billions of dollars. Was the Soviet Union grateful? Not at all; it was hateful, ugly, and threatening instead.

Vast in its land empire and resources, numberless in its armed forces, ruthless in its apparent desire to dominate the world with what the U.S. heartland called "atheistic communism," seen as shameless in its deception, trickery, and international subversions—the Soviet Union was the perfect enemy for twentieth-century Americans. Few doubted that "godless Russia" was ready and able to steal their secrets and to undermine and destroy their institutions; or that American military power alone prevented a Soviet attack using atomic bombs built from stolen U.S. designs. The "evil empire," as President Reagan later called the Soviet behemoth, was a precise description of what many in the United States had believed since—and some before—World War II.

The attitude of the times was double-edged, however. Events had created an evil enemy to be feared and watched lest it somehow overcome honest, good-hearted, but naive Americans. But the victors of World War II (as many Americans persisted in seeing themselves, despite Stalingrad and the Red Army), with their know-how and determination and faultless intentions, could do anything, could go anywhere, could stand for any good cause, and were bound inevitably to triumph (with D-day and Hiroshima as ample evidence). Failure whether in combat or diplomacy could not, therefore, be an *American* failure, for there was no such thing; failure could only result from subversion, espionage by the evil empire, and treason—betrayal in high places.

Faith in a wickedly ingenious enemy, whose reach for evil goals threatened America's inner security, and a blustery over-confidence in U.S. power and resources: the combination made it easy for many Americans to believe that any setback to U.S. interests had to be the consequence of that enemy's unceasing efforts to subvert and control American policy to its own advantage. If even with massive U.S. help, for instance, the anticommunist (and therefore worthy) Chinese nationalists could be driven off the Asian mainland, their defeat could not represent a deficiency either in genuine American efforts or in the nation's anticommunist precepts. Only Soviet subversion, only the duplicity of U.S. officials corrupted by insidious communism—pressured or bought by a foreign power—could explain such failure.

IN THE WAKE of World War II and the early years of the Cold War, such beliefs were strengthened for some Republicans by what seemed to them an obvious connection between communism and organized U.S. Labor.* The latter was then a powerful and controversial force that many nonunion Americans found threatening. Union membership, aided by wartime Democratic administrations' policies, had grown by 50 percent, to about fifteen million; and in the late forties strikes were hamstringing the nation. At one point after World War II, two million workers were on the picket lines. Robert Donovan, in his biography of Harry Truman, summarizes that president's early postwar plight:

> In one year he had seized the coal mines twice; he had seized the railroads; he had seized 134 meat-packing plants; he had seized ninety-one tugboats; he had seized the facilities of twenty-six oil-producing and refining companies; he had seized the Great Lakes Towing Company. . . . [H]e had grappled with huge strikes against General Motors and United States Steel. He had proposed labor legislation only to have Congress ignore it.[4]

Some labor leaders, moreover, *did* have ties to or had expressed sympathy for communists, and some unions *had* suffered infiltration or had been forced to wage battles against

---

* And should have been more legitimately substantiated, had evidence of Soviet wartime and postwar espionage been available. Unfortunately, the Venona transcripts of actual Soviet spy reports were not published until 1995.

communist influence—not always successfully. Many Republicans were persuaded that since the Democrats were
friendly to labor, which heavily supported the party, they were
hospitable to communism as well, and perhaps to Soviet am-
bitions. Republican strategists—out of power since 1933—
reasoned that if Americans feared communism and were wary
of organized labor, a linkage between the two and the Democratic Party not only was plausible but also offered the best
chance for a Republican return to power.

Conservative partisans, in the years during and after the
war, did not hesitate to link aggressive communism and "soft"
Democrats (sometimes justifiably, as with Hiss and a few others). B. Carroll Reece of Tennessee, the Republican national
chairman, denounced the CIO-PAC (organized labor's most
active political arm) in a 1946 radio speech as "the spearhead
of Red reactionism." Later he connected the CIO-PAC to the
Democrats, who had been taken over, Reece said, "by a radical group devoted to Sovietizing the United States." Reece
declared that the 1946 elections were a "fight basically between communism and Republicanism"; and that year a west-
ern Republican conference held in Salt Lake City urged
voters to turn to *their* party for "tried and true Americanism."
Even Taft of Ohio described the Democratic Party as "divided
between communism and Americanism."

The Truman administration came under attack from other
directions as well. In 1946 the president had fired Secretary

of Commerce Henry A. Wallace for attacking Truman foreign policy and for advocating greater cooperation with the Soviet Union. A former vice president who might have become president had FDR not replaced him with Truman, Wallace responded with what ultimately became, in 1948, a leftist third-party challenge.

Meanwhile, more than a few conservative Democrats unreconciled to Franklin Roosevelt and Harry Truman or to the New Deal and Fair Deal—much less to such departures from tradition as Truman's civil rights and foreign-aid programs—also feared that their party had been eroded by subversion (of ideas, at least, and maybe even in fact). "I didn't leave the party of Jefferson," cried the typical Democratic apostate who voted Republican or even supported Strom Thurmond and the Dixiecrats in 1948. "It left me!"

Goaded by Republican charges of being soft on communism and by Democratic defections on his right and left, Truman counterattacked by instituting a loyalty program and by denying Congress access to the administration's security files. Ironically, these policies lent legitimacy to the idea of foreign subversion. *Must be something to hide,* suggested critics from both parties.

THIS FEAR OF SUBVERSION was deeply rooted in American history—with strong precedents including the Great Red Scare following the First World War, the Alien and Sedition

Acts, periodic immigration restrictions, the Haymarket Affair, antisyndicalist laws, the case of Sacco and Vanzetti, and any number of local persecutions.

The Soviet Union's postwar policies exacerbated American mistrust of both "Russia" and "godless communism," which were often equated. Even as internationalist a figure as General Dwight D. Eisenhower, the victor of World War II and later the U.S. Army's chief of staff, found after a few postwar years that his wartime hopes for peaceful cooperation with the Soviet Union had been dashed by Moscow's belligerent actions.

The Soviet Union's rejection of the supposedly equitable Baruch Plan, proposed by the United States for international control of atomic energy,* and Winston Churchill's Iron Curtain speech in Fulton, Missouri, underscored the nation's fear of subversion—regularly fanned by Republican speechmakers, who would ultimately be led by Joseph R. McCarthy.

Nineteen forty-six proved to be a banner year for Republicans. They won the Senate (Joe McCarthy was one of the new faces in the chamber) and gained fifty-five House seats to take control of Congress for the first time since 1933. McCarthy arrived in the Senate without fanfare, particularly in

---

* The Baruch Plan, though it was not so understood by the American public, actually would have left the United States with an atomic monopoly for many years. The Soviets could hardly accept *that*.

comparison to that received by an outstanding class of Republican freshmen entering, across the Capitol, the House of Representatives:

Thruston Morton of Kentucky was to become the party's national chairman; Kenneth Keating of New York, Charles Potter of Michigan, and Norris Cotton of New Hampshire were to move on to the Senate; J. Caleb Boggs would become governor of Delaware and John Lodge, governor of Connecticut (and later ambassador to Spain); John Byrnes of Wisconsin rose to be House Republican leader; and Melvin Laird of Wisconsin was to serve as secretary of defense in the cabinet of the brightest star of them all—Richard M. Nixon of California.

In 1946 Nixon won election to the House over a five-term Democratic veteran, the supposedly leftist Jerry Voorhis. Nixon's tough campaign tactics won him a seat on HUAC and his pursuit of Alger Hiss established him as a "gut-fighter,"* the nation's No. 1 Red hunter. Years would pass before another gut-fighter, Joe McCarthy, began to move in on the latter title.

---

* This identification helped Nixon win a Senate seat in 1950, the Republican vice-presidential nomination in 1952, and the party's presidential nomination in 1960. But the wheel turns; and this lingering reputation may have hurt him with the public when he was accused of dirty tactics in the Watergate scandal, after he finally won the White House in 1968. In 1974 Nixon was the first president forced to resign.

2

★　★　★

THAT JOE MCCARTHY MIGHT someday contend for national fame would have seemed unlikely to those who knew him in 1925 as a seventeen-year-old chicken farmer on his father's land near Appleton, Wisconsin. But those who looked more closely saw a good-natured young Irishman who owned two thousand laying hens, ten thousand broilers, and the beat-up old truck in which he periodically drove to Chicago to market his poultry—a flock that sometimes cost him a thousand dollars or more to feed. Clearly, he was more ambitious than the average seventeen-year-old.[5]

Young McCarthy had only a grade school education; however, he was worldly-wise enough to know that he would never achieve the success he craved—so his family and friends attest—as a boondocks chicken farmer. When he was twenty and an avian disease, coccidiosis, killed thousands of his birds and he suffered a bad case of influenza (foreshadowing the ill health that was to dog him for much of his life), he made no serious effort to rebuild his poultry business.

Instead, he took a clerk's job in Appleton's Cash-Way grocery store, rising quickly to become the store's manager. He was then transferred to manage a new Cash-Way in the village of Manawa, an hour's drive from Appleton. Soon the new store was operating at a profit, and not long after it led the chain in sales—not least because McCarthy, instead of waiting for business behind the counter, often ventured on foot into the countryside, acquainting himself with farmers, inviting them to shop at his store, and laying in a large stock to accommodate them. Honoring his family heritage, he also was a regular attendant at Catholic Mass. McCarthy captivated Manawa with his charm and high spirits—as was to be the case everywhere he became known for years to come.

To an ambitious, hardworking, and talented young man, the small-town grocery business could not have been much more appealing than chicken ranching. At age twenty-one, McCarthy talked himself into Manawa's Little Wolf High School—though it had no legal responsibility to admit anyone over nineteen years of age. He was one of forty-four "freshmen" entering in the fall of 1929; fortunately, the school was inaugurating an experimental program that allowed students to advance at their own pace. McCarthy took advantage of this, requesting the toughest assignments and applying himself so assiduously to his studies that Cash-Way soon told him to quit either the store or the school. The young man quit the store and devoted even his weekends to his studies.

McCarthy also found time to coach boxing—a sport his father had taught him—and to be vice president of the freshman class he soon left behind. In a few months he was a sophomore, in a few more a junior, and by the spring of 1930, Joe McCarthy was one of thirty-nine Little Wolf graduates to receive a diploma. He had done four years of high school work (English, biology, geometry, physics, and all the rest) in only nine months—a feat unprecedented in the twenty-two-year teaching experience of Principal L. B. Hershberger.

THOUGH HE WAS never again a stellar student, Joe McCarthy had proved himself an unusual and gifted young man. In his busy year at Little Wolf, he had even passed a Marquette University correspondence course in advanced algebra—a requirement if, as he wished, he was to be admitted to the university to study engineering. Hershberger finessed another Marquette requirement—four years of high school—by certifying only that McCarthy had completed four years' high school *work*.

After matriculating at Marquette in the fall of 1930, McCarthy spent two relatively routine years in the engineering program. This was in the depth of the Depression, however, and hard times forced him again to display his drive and seemingly limitless energy. He took several jobs at once—

earning a hundred dollars a week at one point by selling fly-paper door to door, a task for which his outgoing personality and Cash-Way sales technique well suited him. After two years at Marquette, he was managing two service stations simultaneously, working ten to twelve hours a day, up to eighty hours a week.

Nevertheless, he did well enough at his studies—though he excelled only in public speaking. McCarthy had been at first an almost hopeless speaker, seemingly unable to face an audience. He developed, however, into an adequate if not compelling orator and distinguished himself on the debating team with his ability to offset a chronic lack of preparation with an instinct for speaking "off the cuff"—a harbinger for the future. Due in part to recurrent sinusitis, however, he spoke in the nasal drone with which millions of TV viewers were to become familiar. And as if foreseeing where he was headed, at the beginning of his junior year McCarthy switched to the Marquette law school—a not uncommon change at the time.

He also joined a rollicking legal students' fraternity, lived in its house, drank a lot of beer, frequently played cards with his "brothers," enjoyed practical jokes played on himself and them, and became a bad but recklessly successful poker player. The frat house marked perhaps McCarthy's first venture into gambling, which was to become—over the table, at the racetrack, in the market—something of a preoccupation.

He also ignored Shakespeare's advice—"neither a borrower nor a lender be"—regularly borrowing money from family and friends, and generously lending what he had to those in need.

Both his generosity and his daring (at poker and in practical jokes) were remembered for years by members of the fraternity, among whom McCarthy was highly popular. They recalled that he was easily angered, too, and always ready to fight—though the storm would quickly pass and he again would be his usual good-humored self.

McCarthy occasionally bluffed his way through law classes, read little, and was never known for an "iron butt" in the library—a reputation that Richard Nixon would earn a few years later at Duke University in North Carolina. McCarthy relied heavily on memorization (at Little Wolf he had displayed an almost-photographic memory), "briefings" from classmates, and sheer energy.

Even so—characteristically, to win a bet—within six hours of graduation and becoming a licensed lawyer in 1935,* McCarthy opened a second-floor law office in the small town of Waupaca, over the quarters of the Waupaca Abstract and Loan Company. But in finishing at Marquette and hanging out his shingle so promptly, he fell deeply into debt—a condition, as remembered by friendly and critical classmates

---

* A Marquette law school graduate automatically became a member of the Wisconsin bar.

alike, that rarely seemed to trouble Joe McCarthy, even in the dark years of the Depression.

THE WORLD OF independent law practice in the 1930s was highly competitive and therefore unprofitable, even for the young charmer most of McCarthy's contemporaries in Waupaca recall. McCarthy threw himself into local civic and charitable activities, supported himself not least at the poker table—where he won a lot of pots by bluffing—and reported a 1935 income of $771.85, not much even by Depression standards.

No wonder, then, that McCarthy accepted a position with another lawyer, Mike G. Eberlein, in the larger nearby town of Shawano. Eberlein had seen McCarthy in court and liked his outgoing style. Soon he made his employee a partner, and it was in Shawano, when McCarthy was twenty-seven, that the future senator's career may be said to have really begun. Not that Joe McCarthy ever brought enough business to Eberlein & McCarthy to be called a rainmaker, but he made a lot of friends, played a lot of cards, developed his courtroom techniques, and became president of Shawano's Young Democratic Club—apparently without protest from the Republican Eberlein. Lawyers, like businessmen, often like to keep a foot on both sides of the political street.

Capitalizing on his YDC position, Joe McCarthy also announced his candidacy in 1936 for district attorney—a position for which he had no visible qualification beyond his law license, his charm, and his ambition. As a Democrat, he was a decided underdog to the Progressive Party* incumbent, one Louis Cattau.

In the primary McCarthy campaigned mostly by hanging signs on his car, with a glad hand for any voter encountered and a proposal to cut the DA's office costs by making it a part-time job. Not surprisingly, as the only man seeking the Democratic nomination, he polled enough votes to win it—but just less than the Republican candidate and almost three thousand fewer than Cattau. But Joe McCarthy had never liked losing, at least since all those chickens died, and these results only seemed to urge him on.

In the general election campaign of 1936, McCarthy emphasized the Democratic Party's accomplishments; praised President Roosevelt inordinately; denounced the Republican platform and the GOP presidential candidate, Alf Landon; and made many speeches in his nasal, Marquette-trained style. But his most effective campaign stroke was distributing a pamphlet accusing Cattau of violating a local ordinance against privately practicing law while acting as DA.

Cattau responded that the charge overstated the case— he had spent little time in separate practice and had earned

---

* The Progressive Party was powerful in Wisconsin in the 1930s, in the tradition of Senator "Fighting Bob" La Follette, one of whose sons, Robert M. La Follette Jr. was then the state's senior U.S. senator.

only a small amount for doing so. But this only acknowledged the violation; and in the general election, Joe McCarthy polled 3,422 votes, a vast improvement over the 577 he had received in the Democratic primary. Cattau still won, with over six thousand votes—but this time it was the Republican candidate who came in last, at 2,842. Tougher, more intense campaigning—with an eye-catching charge against his opponent—had proved effective, as McCarthy surely did not fail to note.

THE POLITICAL BUG, moreover, had bit. As he emerged from the campaign for district attorney, Joe McCarthy seemed to those who knew him "almost totally extroverted, highly aggressive, fun-loving, loud, generous, and constantly in motion."[6] Ambition was bound to assert itself, however, sooner rather than later. At the time it may have been activated by the ill-fated "court-packing" scheme of McCarthy's oft-cited hero, President Franklin D. Roosevelt.

The U.S. Supreme Court had thwarted some of FDR's New Deal measures, ruling them unconstitutional; one of the "nine old men" on its bench, James McReynolds of New York, had said that he would "never resign as long as that crippled son-of-a-bitch is in the White House."[7] McReynolds and five of his Supreme Court colleagues were seventy years old or older, and the three other justices were over sixty. Roosevelt was eager both to move his program forward and to take political revenge; his plan to do so was devised mostly by Attorney

General Homer Cummings. Under Cummings's scheme, the president would appoint six new judges for every one on any federal court who was past seventy years of age, up to a total of fifty new appointees. The expanded Supreme Court was not, however, to exceed fifteen justices. This made it clear that FDR intended to appoint one new justice for each of the six over seventy years old currently serving on the high court; with the three over-sixty justices, this would add up to the specified fifteen.

At first Roosevelt presented this plan not as self-serving politics but as a desire to relieve the workload of aged and infirm jurists. This emphasis may have caught Joe McCarthy's attention; or perhaps it was the defeat of a Shawano County judge by a younger opponent who cited the incumbent's age—or maybe both. In any case, before long McCarthy confided to friends that in 1939 he intended to run against Edgar V. Werner, judge for Wisconsin's Tenth Circuit. The friends scoffed. Judge Werner might be sixty-six years old and none too efficient in his courtroom, they conceded; but he had been twenty years on the bench, a district attorney before that, and Shawano city attorney even earlier. Werner well fitted what traditionally had been desired in Wisconsin's district judges—maturity, long experience, a distinguished record. Joe McCarthy had none of these qualifications and no campaign money. How could he expect to defeat a settled incumbent such as Judge Werner?

His friends' derision seemed, however, to deter McCarthy

less than to spur him on. Besides, as would be the case many times in the future, those friends had underestimated him. If he had no money and no record, he did have a theory and a plan. He thought that people weren't much interested in politicians or political issues but looked for some personal reason to vote for a candidate; and he was sure he could supply that reason by taking advantage of his energy and his likable personality. He would walk and ride through the district's three counties, mostly rural, its many small towns, and its one urban area—Appleton. He would introduce himself to its families, chat with them about their and the district's problems, then send them a personal note suggesting that they were special to him and implicitly asking that he be special to *them*: special enough to vote for.

This plan was not only an innovative approach to winning an underdog race, if it could be won. It also was an early sign of Joe McCarthy's self-confidence—amounting to arrogance. *He* knew he could beat Werner even if no one else thought so; he could do it because he was smarter, harder working, more likable, more in tune with the voters. And if people thought he could not win, laughed at the very idea, then—as in completing four years of high school in nine months—Joe McCarthy would do what no one believed he could do.*

---

* Mike Eberlein, who had hoped to run for the judgeship himself, learned of his partner's intention from a newspaper article. Nevertheless, for years to come Eberlein remained McCarthy's friend, which suggests the latter's personal appeal.

McCarthy's plan might have worked because he pursued it indefatigably, all over the district's three counties*—six and seven days a week, in all kinds of weather—knocking on doors, chatting with voters, swapping stories, kissing babies, sampling farmwives' cooking, even milking a few cows. Once a visit was over, he'd dictate his impressions into a recording device so that an ill-paid young woman in his office could listen to the cylinders and write seemingly personal postcards as a follow-up. She signed McCarthy's name; the young candidate, wearing glasses and looking serious, appeared in a picture on the reverse of the postcard.

All this might have elected McCarthy, but he had another string to his bow—the charge, echoing FDR and the court-packing scheme, that Judge Werner was too old and should be retired. Ironically, Werner had brought this on himself; in the early days of his political career, in an effort to appear more mature, he had proclaimed himself six years older than he was. McCarthy spotted the discrepancy in the *Martindale-Hubbard* directory of lawyers and leaked the word that the judge would be nearly eighty years old at the end of a new term. When Werner countered with the truth of his age, he only compounded the confusion, and McCarthy insisted self-righteously that Werner not be required—or allowed—to serve still another term.

---

* Shawano, Langlade, and Outagamie.

McCarthy also asserted in an ad that Werner had earned nearly $200,000 in office. This was not surprising since the judge had been a public officeholder for thirty-five years. But cited in the middle of the Depression, the lump sum made Werner appear to have fattened his assets at public expense. Numerous voters believed he had. The local press, moreover, printed McCarthy's charges against Werner—and McCarthy's exaggerations of his own legal experience—without checking their accuracy.[8]

For good measure, in the last few days of the campaign, McCarthy sent another round of postcards to those listed in the district's telephone directories. The cards were all hand-written by volunteers who signed the candidate's name, so that McCarthy appeared to have written each message him-self. Many cards again raised the question of Judge Werner's age—should an old man serve another term?

Up to the day of the election, McCarthy continued his rounds of farmhouses and the business streets of the Tenth District's many small towns,* displaying his good-fellow per-sonality, greeting voters, asking for their help—and, with his remarkable memory, often amazing and flattering them by using their first names.

On April 5, 1939, when the votes were counted in the

---

* This, too, was a rather innovative tactic in 1939. Today it is a shibboleth of political campaigning to continue running until the last moment.

nonpartisan election, the *Appleton Post-Gazette* recorded "one of the most astonishing upsets" in Tenth District history: Mc-Carthy, 15,160; Werner, 11,154; and a third candidate, 9,071. In an ironic twist on the "age issue," Joe McCarthy—only four years out of law school—became the youngest district judge ever elected in Wisconsin. (And also one of the most indebted: it took a secret seven thousand–dollar bank loan to pay off McCarthy's campaign borrowings.)[9]

Was victory the fruit of the relentless energy with which an upstart candidate pursued his campaign strategy? Or was it brought about by the innovative nature of the strategy itself? Did the third candidate draw off votes from Judge Werner? Or perhaps the election was won by the large corps of volunteers who supported (some after initial hesitation) their friend Joe, and who would in many cases remain his backers through all the controversial years ahead? To some extent, of course, the campaign only provided another example of a familiar story—a young and vigorous candidate surprising and outgunning an older, perhaps complacent opponent.

How much McCarthy's victory relied on his devious (but not exactly false) charges against Werner will never be precisely determined. Werner thought the charges contributed heavily to his defeat; after the election he and his backers demanded an investigation of McCarthy's spending (the victor had reported only $1,221.58 in campaign expenses, an obvious underaccounting) and his misrepresentation of the judge's age. McCarthy survived the lengthy investigation that followed and took his seat on the bench in 1940. But had a pattern been set?

It may be too much to assert that it had been. Nearly seventy years later, however, it seems plausible to suggest that the seeds of what came to be known as McCarthyism were first sown in Wisconsin's Tenth District judgeship campaign in 1939.

ON TAKING OVER the district court, McCarthy found that Edgar Werner—whether or not because of his disputed age—had indeed been less than efficient, leaving a backlog of nearly 250 cases. Judge McCarthy attacked it with characteristic energy, keeping court open twelve hours a day, working Saturdays, once trying forty cases in forty days, reaching off-the-bench settlements when possible, and granting uncontested divorces in a few minutes. The backlog disappeared within months.

Judge McCarthy acquitted himself reasonably well, showing particular concern for the children of parents seeking divorces. He did not know much law, but litigants and lawyers alike praised his promptitude, common sense, and good humor (though, owing to his chronic sinusitis, smoking was not allowed in the McCarthy courtroom). However, in a case involving milk sales by the Quaker Dairy Company of Appleton considerable trouble arose. The company had sold milk below the price set by the state Department of Agriculture; McCarthy's ruling in favor of Quaker appeared to allow the company to violate state law, and the state supreme court reversed his decision, citing actions that "constituted an abuse of judicial authority." Whereupon McCarthy—who in the future would be willing to defy two presidents of the United States—*again* ruled in favor of the company. This time the state did not appeal, and the public appeared to favor the judge's actions—or at least Quaker's low milk price.

Though the law may have been McCarthy's profession, at this point the gaming table was more nearly his livelihood. He played cards frequently, once all night until the time came to open his courtroom in the morning. One evening at the Racine Elks Club, he won two thousand dollars. But on a vacation in Biloxi, Mississippi, he lost so much at roulette and in the slot machines that he had to wire his friend and court reporter, Pat Howlett, for funds. With such habits, Joe McCarthy, not surprisingly, became at about this time a heavy drinker.

Politics was not forgotten. McCarthy frequently exchanged district court responsibilities with other judges, in this way gathering hundreds of new names and addresses from all over the state to enter into his Dictaphone. He accepted as many speaking invitations as he could, from anywhere in Wisconsin, and was known to drive from Appleton to nearby towns to give speeches during trial recesses.

The political bug had bitten deep, and soon McCarthy was telling Urban Van Susteren and other friends that he aimed to run for the U.S. Senate—somehow, sometime, date unspecified. Confidants were dumfounded, but—in view of the 1939 campaign—this time no one scoffed. Some did point out that state law prevented a sitting judge from running for any other office; McCarthy, moreover, was still a Democrat, which was not an advantage in Wisconsin. Besides, both of the state's U.S. senators, Robert La Follette Jr. ("Young Bob") and Alexander Wiley, seemed well entrenched.

McCarthy again brushed aside all objections—save one. On December 7, 1941, the Japanese struck Pearl Harbor and U.S. participation in World War II became a fact that he could not dismiss. By early 1942 young American men were volunteering by the thousands. Van Susteren, who was joining the army, suggested to his friend McCarthy that the Marine Corps offered more glamour. Apparently for this reason—a judge could have been exempt from the draft—Joseph R. McCarthy enlisted in the corps on June 4, 1942, in Milwaukee. He was thirty-three years old.

McCarthy had applied for a commission and was appointed first lieutenant on July 29. He was sworn in at that rank on August 4 and never served a day as an enlisted man. For the rest of his life, nevertheless, McCarthy claimed that he had joined up as a private, sometimes saying a "buck private," and had *earned* his promotion to officer's rank. He made this claim wholesale, in campaign literature, later in the *Congressional Directory,* in *Who's Who in America,* and anywhere else that mattered. The truth was not disclosed until 1951.

Why the exaggeration—an outright lie? Because the buck-private story was politically advantageous in a nation of buck privates, and because Joe McCarthy had by no means given up his political ambition when he donned the uniform. In the 1940s, in fact, the uniform was politically necessary clothing—and an identification that self-confident Joe Mc-Carthy was sure he could turn into a plus.

McCARTHY DID NOT RESIGN from the bench but took a leave of absence and arranged for other circuit judges to fill in for him while he was in service. For the rest of 1942 and in early 1943, he served at various marine posts—Quantico, Virginia; Camp Lejeune, North Carolina; and El Centro, California. He also attended the Army Intelligence School in Harrisburg, Pennsylvania. In March 1943 he became Captain McCarthy, the intelligence officer of marine dive-bomber squadron VMSB-235. With its forty pilots and other personnel, he arrived overseas, at Pearl Harbor, on March 31, 1943.

After two months' further training at Ewa, a nearby marine base in Hawaii, the squadron embarked on the seaplane tender *Chandeleur* for the South Pacific. Captain McCarthy was a popular man—witty, intelligent, a scintillating conversationalist, and enterprising. Another marine recalled that the former judge had "three trunks marked 'office supplies—squadron 235' and all three supplies were liquid."[10] He also practiced, aboard ship, his bad but daring poker, often bluffing his way to substantial pots.

The *Chandeleur* crossed the equator on June 22, and McCarthy was initiated as a "polliwog" in a raucous "shellback" ceremony. At one point, descending a ladder with a bucket hanging from his right foot, McCarthy fell backward and suffered a fracture of that foot. Later, when the cast was removed, acid used in the process burned McCarthy's ankle and left a large scar.

Despite later claims, these were the only physical injuries Joe McCarthy suffered in the Marine Corps or while serving overseas. He never received or deserved a Purple Heart. In July 1943, however, Wisconsin newspapers carried a marine press release announcing that Captain McCarthy had suffered leg and facial injuries requiring hospitalization; in November another press release stated that he had been wounded in action. After the war McCarthy sometimes walked with a limp and was heard saying that he carried ten pounds of shrapnel in his leg. (He later denied having made such a statement.) He was also heard on occasion to claim that he had been in a plane that ground-looped and burned on landing. Records show that VMSB-235 suffered only one such accident—and Joe McCarthy was not aboard the ill-fated craft.

In fact, the political moniker he liked and later promoted—
"Tailgunner Joe"—had little basis in fact. The squadron was
based in the combat zone, at Guadalcanal, and its flight missions were often exceedingly dangerous. But McCarthy's
work was on the ground, briefing and debriefing pilots before
and after their missions and studying their combat photos. He
managed, at the same time, to operate several profitable sidelines, bringing in liquor and other goodies for the squadron,
and therefore remained a popular figure with his comrades.
He talked himself into quite a few combat missions. On several occasions he was under fire, but he was excluded from
the most dangerous missions and usually allowed only on
"milk runs." Pilots wanted a real tail gunner, not an enthusi-
astic amateur, when they flew against difficult targets such as
the Japanese base at Rabaul.

In 1944, running for the U.S. Senate in Wisconsin while
stationed on Guadalcanal (about which, more later), Mc-
Carthy let it be known in the state that he had flown fourteen
combat missions. By 1946, when he was back in Wisconsin,
the claim had grown to seventeen missions. In 1951, when he
was a famous senator and a national figure, he said his combat missions numbered thirty-two—a figure accepted by a
Marine Corps well aware of McCarthy's office and political
stature. The corps then awarded McCarthy the Distinguished
Flying Cross (which is reserved for those who have flown at
least twenty-five combat missions) as well as an Air Medal and
four stars. In his log Major Glenn Todd, McCarthy's com-

manding officer at Guadalcanal, had certified only eleven such missions for Tailgunner Joe—and flew only fourteen himself.

After the war McCarthy often rebutted doubts about his wartime exploits by citing an official commendation signed by Admiral Chester Nimitz in the spring of 1944 (just before McCarthy ran for the Senate from Guadalcanal against the incumbent, Alexander Wiley). The Nimitz citation mentioned injuries and "courageous devotion to duty" in keeping with the highest traditions. Major Todd did not remember writing the letter of recommendation on which the citation was based but did recall that wartime intelligence officers were often assigned to write such letters. Nimitz received thousands of them during the war and routinely issued the recommended citations. Therefore, McCarthy's must be regarded with a skeptical eye.

These exaggerations—lies—about his wartime service were directed toward Joe McCarthy's consuming ambition, undiverted by a mere war, to be elected to the U.S. Senate. By 1944, with Senator Wiley up for reelection and McCarthy serving his country overseas (while evoking ample publicity* for doing so), the time seemed auspicious—not perhaps to win but at least to build a solid base upon which to run

---

* McCarthy saw to it that several photos of him in flying gear, standing by a dive bomber or posing with machine guns, appeared in the Wisconsin press along with stories about "the flying judge." He filed for the Senate primary by mail in April 1944 and immediately began to send back campaign literature.

against Senator La Follette in 1946. Besides, friends in the Wisconsin legislature—McCarthy had not been entering all those names in his Dictaphone for nothing—had repealed the state law barring a judge from running for other office.

McCarthy's prewar investments in the stock market, moreover, had paid off by 1944; for the first time in his life, Joe McCarthy had some real money—about forty thousand dollars in an account with Wayne Hummer and Company, a brokerage firm in Appleton. As for being a Democrat, that was a mere inconvenience. McCarthy switched to the Republican Party with no more hesitation than when he had claimed heroic wartime service.

ON JULY 13, 1944—while VMSB-235 was on its fourth combat tour, flying missions against New Ireland and New Britain—Wisconsin newspapers announced that Judge-Captain Joseph R. McCarthy had landed on the West Coast and was on his way to Wisconsin. To facilitate his primary campaign against Wiley, McCarthy had wangled a transfer to the Marine Air Fleet in San Diego, a move that automatically yielded him a fifteen-day leave.

After so many machinations, it might be supposed that McCarthy—the upstart, the innovator, the daring underdog—would somehow pull out another victory. But he didn't. The Republican state leadership was solidly behind Wiley. McCarthy's personal campaigning—though he was a marine in uniform—was less effective than usual, perhaps because he didn't truly expect to win. The old charge of his ineligibility to run was raised again.* McCarthy won a few newspaper endorsements and his network of friends rallied to the cause; still, Wiley won the primary easily, as expected. McCarthy may have taken some comfort from the nearly eighty thousand votes he did win, particularly from carrying all three counties within his old judicial district.

The day after the primary, McCarthy returned to California and to the marines, his fifteen-day leave having expired. He did not, however, neglect his political and party duty—or his future—in Wisconsin: he left a letter urging his supporters to vote for Wiley, and he sent Wiley a list of McCarthy campaign leaders. Wiley does not appear to have called on any of them.

In October, though McCarthy was eligible for further overseas duty, he applied for a four-month leave to attend to urgent duties at home. The Marine Corps gave him the option of resigning his commission. He accepted on December 11, 1944,† and in February 1945 he was back on the bench

---

* McCarthy's campaign effectively established that no state could prescribe the qualifications for a U.S. senator, a federal responsibility. But the charge continued to haunt him.

† Though it was not necessarily his motivation, McCarthy therefore avoided possible participation in the return to the Philippines and the fighting at Saipan and Okinawa.

in Appleton—still wearing his marine uniform and captain's bars.

Despite his exaggerated claims and self-inspired publicity, McCarthy had served without official blemish in one of the war's most active combat zones. Not least for that reason, in April 1945 Tailgunner Joe was reelected to his Tenth District judgeship without opposition. The stage was set for the 1946 Senate election, and Joe McCarthy's part in the play had already been written.

3

On March 17, 1946, in Portage, Wisconsin, at a convention of the state's Progressive Party, Senator Robert M. La Follette Jr., scion of a famous dynasty and one of the more respected men in Washington, announced that as expected he would seek reelection. His next statement shocked the nation, the state, and especially his Progressive audience: he would run as a Republican.

The Republicans were by far the majority party in Wisconsin, but local political analysts were surprised anyway. For most of the century, state Republicans had been divided between conservative Stalwarts and more liberal Progressives—the latter led since 1902 by Young Bob La Follette's family. Its patriarch, the brilliant reformer Robert M. La Follette Sr. (Old Bob), had been the state's governor and a third-party presidential candidate and had served as a U.S. senator until his death in 1925. Robert Junior had been elected to complete his father's last term and then won three Senate terms in his own right. His brother, Philip La Follette, had been governor of Wisconsin from 1931 to 1933 and from 1935 to 1939.

The split among Republicans had been so deep that in 1934 the La Follettes abandoned the party, formally organized the Progressives as a separate entity, and cooperated with the Roosevelt administration—even backing FDR in the 1936 presidential campaign. The Progressives, rather than the lack-luster state Democratic Party, provided the real opposition to the GOP in Wisconsin.

After 1938, as the New Deal faltered and Roosevelt turned more completely to foreign affairs, Young Bob became a strong isolationist and the family tried to form a *national* Progressive Party. It failed to catch on, Philip was ousted as governor, Wisconsin Progressives suffered defeats in 1942 and 1944, and the old Stalwart faction took firm command of the Wisconsin Republican Party. The Stalwart leader was Thomas C. Coleman, a wealthy former businessman who hated the La Follettes and being called "Boss," in roughly that order. Boss, however, was what Coleman was since he also controlled the Republican Voluntary Committee, the party's financial base.

Coleman had vowed to resist the La Follettes' return to his party and termed Young Bob's move "pure expediency." For that reason, some Wisconsin political buffs thought Robert Junior had made a mistake by not remaining a Progressive or, with approval from Washington, even styling himself a Democrat.

Coleman, however, had no candidate of his own to pit against Young Bob in a Republican primary—no one but the former marine, Judge Joseph R. McCarthy of Appleton, a recent Democrat with no known views on the major issues, little experience, and not much else to recommend him. A hard-eyed pro like Tom Coleman was not impressed that McCarthy was a war veteran and an indefatigable campaigner with unlimited self-confidence; in fact, the Republican boss distrusted the bombastic McCarthy's social skills, fearing the judge would be no match for the sophisticated La Follette.

As usual, McCarthy was being underestimated by those who knew nothing about his career at Little Wolf High School. For one thing, McCarthy had shrewdly set himself by Tom Coleman's side, denouncing La Follette and his family's history of what McCarthy called party destruction. For another, the young Appleton judge had formed a close alliance with one Loyal Eddy, a Milwaukee salesman who, with Coleman's backing, was trying to form a Wisconsin Young Republican Club.

With his customary relentlessness, McCarthy dogged Eddy's footsteps about the state, and in his practiced backslapping manner, he became acquainted with thousands of potential young Republicans. He committed their names to

his Dictaphone or to his exceptional memory, adding many of
them to the supporters he had collected during his judgeship
and 1944 Senate campaigns. When the Young Republicans
were formally organized at a convention in Eau Claire, the
Stalwarts may have been surprised to find that the keynote
speaker was none other than the hard-charging judge and ex-
marine, Tailgunner Joe. In fact, at that meeting McCarthy
had to beg off from being nominated for state vice president,
explaining confidently to the Young Republicans that he was
going to be elected to the U.S. Senate.

In his speech McCarthy even disclosed, for a change,
some of his views. He was against bureaucracy and the Truman administration but favored a voluntary army and higher
prices for farm products. He also proposed a cautious set of
regulations on union activity—carefully not too antilabor. In
foreign affairs he feared U.S. bungling had squandered U.S.
gains from World War II. This rather typically Republican
speech, of course, was aimed at Coleman and the Stalwarts
as much as at those actually in the audience. But many of
McCarthy's actual hearers featured the veteran's "Ruptured
Duck"* on their lapels, side by side with a "Judge Joe" button.

Less than two weeks later, Coleman's Voluntary Committee met at Oshkosh. McCarthy and Eddy saw to it that
Young Republicans made up about 20 percent of the voting

---

* A lapel button awarded to World War II veterans.

delegates. They also blanketed the meeting with letters urging an endorsement for McCarthy's Senate candidacy. The
judge, while attending to his duties on the bench, was as
usual campaigning hard in dozens of cities and towns. Other
aspirants dropped out, one by one, some under disputed circumstances.* When Voluntary Committee plenary sessions
opened, Joe McCarthy was the only serious candidate remaining in the Republican primary race to oppose La Follette.†

Tom Coleman had been around long enough to read the
writing on the wall—and, more importantly, to see the Young
Republicans, Loyal Eddy, and McCarthy assiduously working
the hotel halls and ballrooms in Oshkosh. Some influential
Stalwarts also had come around to supporting the former marine; having no real alternative, Coleman eventually did, too.
The Voluntary Committee endorsed McCarthy on the first
ballot, 2,328 to 238, and he accepted the backing with a
plausible promise:

"I don't claim to be more brilliant than the next man, but
I have always claimed that I have worked harder. I am going
to work harder."[11]

---

* It was reported, for instance, that Walter Kohler dropped out after Mc-
  Carthy threatened to make an issue of Kohler's divorce, which might have
  ruined his chances with Catholic voters.
† The Voluntary Committee could endorse a primary candidate, but the official Republican Party could not.

Those who knew Joe McCarthy had little doubt that the judge would do just that.

MOST OBSERVERS, IN FACT, believed McCarthy had no choice but to "work harder," as opinion polls gave the far better-known La Follette a substantial primary lead. But, as promised, McCarthy kept up his headlong personal campaigning, crisscrossing Wisconsin countless times, working grueling days to meet and impress as many voters as he could (while still running his court). It soon was apparent that he had a particular appeal for young people, many of whom were also veterans. McCarthy bore down hard on his war record,* offered strong support to organized labor, and severely criticized La Follette's isolationism.

One effective campaign tool was a pamphlet McCarthy personally entitled *The Newspapers Say . . .* (nobody would read it, the candidate told his campaign manager, Urban Van Susteren, if it were labeled simply *McCarthy for Senator*). The brochure emphasized McCarthy's youth and his judicial and military records but had little to say about issues. Thousands of copies were distributed—with Coleman footing the bill— and polls showed that many voters responded favorably. Also boosting McCarthy's chances was a team of about a thousand

---

* Apparently, no one in the press or the opposition seriously investigated his claims, most of which would have been vulnerable to inquiry.

Young Republican "Flying Badgers"; they chartered airplanes to distribute McCarthy literature, covering—in the closing days of the primary—virtually every Wisconsin town of five hundred or more people. This was an exciting and innovative campaign technique in the 1940s.

For his part, Young Bob did not seem to take McCarthy seriously—perhaps because, as some friends believed, the moody and introverted La Follette, though devoted to his work in the Senate, did not much care whether he won or lost a fourth term. He already had had a close run in the 1940 election. A serious, reclusive man, he was not good at meeting and greeting voters; at one point in his senatorial career he had lived in Virginia, and for many years he had visited Wisconsin infrequently. Preoccupied with legislation in Washington, he did not return to the state in 1946 until about a week before the primary on August 3; and though McCarthy repeatedly challenged him to debate, La Follette refused.*

Young Bob was strongly anticommunist, but his isolationism had hurt him in some quarters. He also suffered sharp criticism from Democrats, particularly former Progressives, who felt spurned by his Republican turn and the occasion he chose to take it. Regular Democrats also preferred to face the untried McCarthy rather than an incumbent in the general

---

* Only seven years later, in 1953, Robert M. La Follette Jr. took his own life.

election. In the tangle of Wisconsin politics, La Follette wors-
ened his troubles by unnecessarily endorsing a candidate running against the incumbent Republican governor, Walter
Goodland. This prompted Coleman to throw his full weight
behind Governor Goodland. The governor, formerly a neutral
in the Senate primary, returned Coleman's favor by supporting Joe McCarthy, making the judge the beneficiary of Young
Bob's unwise gubernatorial endorsement.

In these circumstances, with only a third of eligible voters turning out for the primary, one of the leading lights of
the U.S. Senate—a well-known and widely respected national figure, the inheritor of a formidable political tradition—
was narrowly defeated by a small-town circuit judge with a
hoked-up war record, whose very eligibility to run had been
strongly questioned. In the end Republicans chose Joe Mc-
Carthy by 207,935 to 202,557 for Young Bob La Follette.*

A DEMOCRATIC CANDIDATE, former congressman Howard
McMurray, still blocked Joe McCarthy's ambition, dating to
the 1930s, to be a member of the U.S. Senate. Underfinanced
and a minority-party candidate, McMurray nevertheless proved

---

* Representative Estes Kefauver of Tennessee wrote La Follette to say that he
had "never felt worse about a defeat. . . . You were one of the two or three
most valuable men in Congress." Thomas C. Reeves, *The Life and Times of
Joe McCarthy* (Lanham, MD: Madison Books, 1997), p. 93.

to be no pushover. He revived the charges that McCarthy as a state judge was ineligible to run and had granted "quickie" divorces for political advantage. In a series of angry debates, McMurray showed himself nearly a match for McCarthy in innuendo, distortion, and invective. Some newspapers also unearthed the Quaker Dairy story that McCarthy had managed to survive years earlier.

With the war over and FDR in his grave, however, 1946 was a Republican year. The GOP regained the House of Representatives for the first time since 1933 and added to its strength in the Senate and in state houses. At age thirty-eight, Joseph Raymond McCarthy, not long before a chicken farmer and grocery clerk, became the youngest U.S. senator in the nation, defeating Howard McMurray by nearly a quarter million votes and carrying seventy of Wisconsin's seventy-one counties.

To Lawrence Eklund, a veteran *Milwaukee Journal* reporter and later the paper's Washington bureau chief, McCarthy offered his victory mantra. He might not be any smarter "than the next fellow," McCarthy said, "but I work twice as hard, and that's what I intend to do in Washington."

THIS TIME, HOWEVER, McCarthy's confidence was not met with success. His amiable manner gave him for a while a certain popularity among other senators, and his bachelor status brought a quick entrée into Washington drawing rooms (where, as elsewhere, hostesses were on the lookout for an "extra man"). He also made some influential friends outside the Senate, not least the wealthy former ambassador to Great Britain Joseph P. Kennedy.[12] Otherwise, the hardworking, fast-risen star of Wisconsin politics failed to make a strong impression in his new role or on his new colleagues.[13]

McCarthy managed in a battle over postwar sugar rationing to champion housewives' need for larger allotments— but also to earn the hostility of senators Charles Tobey of New Hampshire and Ralph Flanders of Vermont, later a mortal enemy. As a member of the Banking and Currency Committee, McCarthy took a mostly constructive interest in the late 1940s housing shortage but temporarily alienated the putative 1948 Republican presidential candidate, Robert Taft, a conservative with a soft spot for public housing. McCarthy leaned more toward the conventional housing market, and, in chairing a touring subcommittee that took testimony on housing problems, he began to exhibit something of the impatience and brusque demeanor for which, in his later anticommunist hearings, he was to become famous.

What had happened to the good-natured fellow who had barnstormed so successfully through Wisconsin politics? It is hard to escape the impression that after his besting of Tom Coleman and Young Bob La Follette, the new senator's high opinion of his own brains and talent had turned into arrogance, while his unheralded arrival in Washington and the

greater attention paid to more glamorous Republicans entering the House of Representatives had disappointed him after
his long effort to get to the Senate. If McCarthy attributed
his negligible legislative record or influence to envy and lack
of appreciation among his colleagues, it would not have been
the first time an offended man looked for the fault in others
rather than in himself. Perhaps, too, McCarthy was overly
savoring the prominence of his important position and the
publicity and perquisites that went with it.

McCarthy, who had a lifelong hunger for money, had accepted ten thousand dollars from the Lustron Corporation for
writing—or at least claiming authorship of—a booklet on
housing and how veterans in particular could obtain it. There
appears to be little validity to charges that McCarthy lobbied
for Lustron in return. He was properly open to criticism, however, and received plenty of it, for accepting a fee from a company in an industry overseen by the Banking and Currency
Committee. Like many politicians and even Supreme Court
justices, then and now, McCarthy seemed remarkably oblivi-
ous to the *appearance* of conflict of interest.

A blow not of his own making befell McCarthy when in
1948 the Democrats regained control of the Senate in the
same election that unexpectedly returned Harry Truman to
the White House. The Democrats' Senate victory relegated
McCarthy to the minority. Any early popularity he had at-
tained soon faded, moreover, due in part to his squabbles

with Tobey, Flanders, Taft, and others, and to his all-too-evident disregard for Senate rules and traditions. This was a personal and political misjudgment of the sort McCarthy had seldom made in Wisconsin in his hungrier years.

As it was, McCarthy's disdain for Senate procedures had so offended Burnet R. Maybank, Democrat of South Carolina and the new chairman of Banking and Currency, that Maybank refused to take the chair if Joe McCarthy remained on the committee. Republican colleagues unceremoniously dumped the Wisconsin senator to the Committee on Expenditures in the Executive Department and to its subcommittee on the District of Columbia—the Senate's least prestigious panel.

McCarthy appealed to Taft, who, predictably, did nothing to help the belligerent newcomer. Rather than remaining patiently in obscurity, the bumptious McCarthy tried to fight back. He insisted that the Executive Expenditures investigating subcommittee on which he sat be empowered to look into an explosive situation involving the so-called Malmédy Massacre during World War II.

In 1946 seventy-three former Nazi troopers had been found guilty of an atrocity, near Malmédy in Belgium, against U.S. troops and Belgian civilians; forty-three of the troopers were sentenced to death. General Lucius D. Clay, the postwar military governor of Germany, commuted thirty-one of the death sentences. But in December 1948 an American Quaker group, the National Council for the Prevention of

War, charged that the accused Nazis had been subjected to torture and mistreatment. An army study commission had already recommended commutation of the sentences of the remaining twelve condemned troopers on grounds that the Germans had acted in the heat of a ferocious battle and that some doubt existed about the legal proceedings by which they had been judged. Articles in *Time* magazine, the *New York Times,* the *Progressive* in Wisconsin, and other publications sparked a furor that echoed into the Senate. When General Clay commuted six more death sentences but ordered the final six carried out, even more doubt was created; Secretary of the Army Kenneth Royall stayed all the capital penalties pending congressional investigation.

The Senate Armed Services Committee first refused jurisdiction, then seized it, shutting out the Executive Expenditures Committee. This infuriated McCarthy anew and opened a rift between him and Millard Tydings of Maryland, the Democratic chairman of Armed Services. Tydings was to become another implacable enemy—and eventually a political victim of the future Red hunter. In 1949, as Armed Services chairman, Tydings appointed a Republican, Raymond Baldwin of Connecticut, to head a subcommittee inquiry into Malmédy and its aftermath.

As a courtesy to the Executive Expenditures Committee, Baldwin invited McCarthy to observe the hearings and agreed to share with him all documentation and information—generosity he soon came to regret.

McCarthy studied the case, including the Germans' charges against their American prosecutors, and apparently became convinced that the Nazi troopers had been improperly tried and treated. No doubt the senator was influenced by the large German population of Wisconsin and by the political support of a Wisconsin industrialist with a long pro-German record, one Walter Harnischfeger. Tom Korb, an old law school chum of McCarthy's, had become Harnischfeger's general counsel; in 1949 he took a leave of absence to become McCarthy's unpaid assistant.

The Wisconsin senator plunged ahead with his usual energy and self-confidence and became virtually a subcommittee member. But his rude, brusque behavior, his criticisms of the subcommittee, and his bullying of witnesses—far different from his old courtroom behavior in Appleton—eventually turned Baldwin, too, into a critic and an enemy. McCarthy was certain—he said often and loudly—that the Baldwin panel was determined upon a "whitewash" of the American prosecutors and the army in general.* In fact, one prosecutor whose conduct was at issue *had* become a member of Baldwin's Connecticut law firm.

As the hearings progressed, however, testimony began to make the German case—McCarthy's adopted case—sound less convincing and more like a postconviction effort for

---

* It seems possible that army-McCarthy hostility, which would be prominent in later years, began here.

clemency. The American prosecutors had made substantial mistakes—allowing victims, for example, to interrogate the accused troopers—but no evidence supported allegations that they had tortured, beaten, or starved prisoners (charges that foreshadowed the Abu Ghraib scandal in Iraq in 2003 and 2004).

McCarthy had made much of an allegation that the Nazi defendants had been kicked or kneed in the groin with "irreparable damage" resulting, a charge that had first appeared in an article by E. L. van Roden. But van Roden, a former Orphans' Court judge in Pennsylvania who had been a member of a civilian commission investigating the Malmédy case, exploded this charge when he was called to testify to the Baldwin subcommittee. He admitted that the article had been written by a member of a pacifist, isolationist group using his byline! He knew nothing, he said, about anyone being kicked or kneed in the groin.

McCarthy should have been silenced by this and other revelations, but he was only briefly deflated.[14] He continued to insist that Baldwin and the subcommittee were trying to whitewash the army and its prosecutors; in effect, he accepted as truth the unsupported affidavits of former SS troopers against the sworn testimony of U.S. Army officers, whom he frequently accused of lying. But when subcommittee members traveled to Germany—without McCarthy, perhaps having had enough of him—again they found no evidence to justify the sensational charges against the American prosecutors.

During the Washington sessions, McCarthy's shrewd-
ness and his knowledge of the Germans' side of the case
sometimes could be glimpsed in his questioning of witnesses. More often, in his zeal he berated all who disagreed
with him, including subcommittee members and Chairman
Baldwin; he recklessly hurled charges of lying, perjury, and
cover-up; threatened to bolt when displeased; and frequently
tried Baldwin's patience. The record shows that the Connecticut senator continued—probably not without struggle—
to be eminently fair.

On one occasion, when McCarthy requested that a witness be subjected to a lie-detector test, he was overruled. Mc-
Carthy angrily shouted that this decision *proved* that a
whitewash was in progress—although, as a lawyer and former
judge, he should have known that polygraph tests, however
impressive in headlines, are frequently inaccurate and therefore inadmissible in many jurisdictions.

Even after the Baldwin panel issued a convincing final
report citing evidence that refuted the German charges, Mc-
Carthy continued to call the panel's work a whitewash. The
Armed Services Committee not only accepted the subcommittee's final report; it also rebuked McCarthy by passing a
resolution of full confidence in Raymond Baldwin. Signato-
ries included men at the heart of the Senate "club"—Richard
Russell of Georgia, Harry F. Byrd of Virginia, Leverett Salton-
stall of Massachusetts. Even Styles Bridges of New Hamp-

shire and William Knowland of California, Republicans who would later enthusiastically back Joe McCarthy's Red hunt, added their names.

THUS, ON FEBRUARY 9, 1950, McCarthy's status in the Senate and the GOP was not the highest. But that was not known to the Republican faithful who turned out in Wheeling, West Virginia, to hear the senator speak at their traditional Lincoln Day dinner. And that night, perhaps not fully understanding in historical terms what he was doing, McCarthy appealed powerfully to the less visible side of the two-faced American personality—to the nation's fears rather than to its boasts, fears as evident in West Virginia as in any state.

Praising the flag in the Lincoln Day tradition, McCarthy also invoked the insecurity that could so easily afflict the American psyche—the dark unease that had been stirred by Soviet belligerence, by the outing of real and imagined spies, by the new threat of an atomic attack on the supposedly impregnable American heartland, by seemingly inexplicable events in China, and by decades of Republican charges* of

---

* Some of these allegations were shown to be true or substantial by the opening of the Venona Project in 1995. Venona disclosed the texts of thousands of World War II–era messages from the KGB station in New York to the home office in Moscow. The messages, all long preceding McCarthy's charges, were decrypted by U.S. code breakers but kept secret for forty years.

communist tendencies in the New Deal and the Fair Deal, organized labor, and the Democratic Party.

Speaking at the right time and with the right words, Mc-
Carthy tapped into a current already flowing and loosed it
into a flood. He had not expected any great response, and he
knew little about communist subversion other than its political potential. He was always more eager and anxious than
sophisticated, and his research was sloppy and his charges
slippery; but his instinct was sound, if after the fact, and his
political aim was unerring. As word of his charges spread
across the nation and particularly to Washington, a number
of Senate Republicans seem to have decided that, though
brash and generally unpopular, McCarthy might be a new
leader for their party, one who could boost the anticommunist issue into a winning orbit. And what is politics about if
not winning?

These Republicans must have been impressed, not by
McCarthy's talk of Reds in the State Department (mostly old
stuff), but by the excitement he had aroused in the country
and by his publicity stunt in telegraphing Truman—two days
after the Wheeling speech—with a demand that the president open the administration's loyalty and security files to
Congress (more old stuff but delivered this time to the desk
where the buck stopped). If Truman kept the files closed,
McCarthy had lectured the president, the Democratic Party
would be labeled "the bedfellow of international commu-

nism." Since many Americans believed that communists practiced "free love" (among other iniquities), the word "bedfellow" even rang faintly of homoeroticism.

SCARCELY A WEEK AFTER firing off these rockets, the new sensation—suddenly a center of media and political attention—again showed more sluggish Republicans how to make lemonade out of desiccated political lemons. In a lengthy Senate speech on February 20, McCarthy—again relying on no original research—spellbound the chamber and the crowded galleries (a measure of the interest he had created) by merely reading in his nasal monotone from a distorted but recognizable version of the so-called Lee List.

This collection of dossiers of past, present, and would-be State Department employees, compiled in 1947 by a House investigative team headed by an old communist hunter named Robert E. Lee, had been widely available around Capitol Hill for three years. It had even appeared in the *Congressional Record*. But McCarthy blithely informed his audience that he had crashed through State Department secrecy to put together a new text describing current espionage and treason in Foggy Bottom.

No matter that some listening senators must have known they were hearing warmed-over (and mostly unproven) information; no matter that some senators may even have been trying to follow McCarthy's oratory with their own readily

available copies of the Lee List.* The drama was the thing—
bravely purloined data on specific administration pinkos and,
worse, being read aloud on the Senate floor by an unafraid
defender of American values.

Actually, only forty-six of the roughly one hundred persons Robert E. Lee had reported on in 1947 remained in the
State Department in 1950—and all forty-six had been targets
of full FBI field investigations. Nevertheless, McCarthy managed by innuendo, omission, distortion, misstatement, and exaggeration both subtle and outrageous to be convincing in his
assertion that the State Department was a sinkhole of subversion. As only one example of his mendacious use of the Lee
List, McCarthy did not mention that one of the dossiers he
cited included a memo stating that *no information* had been
developed "tending to affect adversely the subject's loyalty."[15]
With what must have been tongue in cheek, he even assured
his hearers: "I am not evaluating the information myself. I am
only giving what is in the files"[16]—a blatant deception of the
kind that later he was often to impose on the nation.

Deception, distortion, exaggeration—all are forms of
lying; and in any form, lying is to be deplored and condemned, especially when done by public persons in public
forums. By February 1950, only a decade after Joe Mc-
Carthy's use of the "age issue" against Judge Werner in Wis-

---

* McCarthy had made this more difficult by renumbering or omitting some
of Lee's cases.

consin, lying seems to have become a part of Senator Mc-
Carthy's stock in trade.

And yet . . . and yet . . . a half century after that February
20 speech, it is possible also to see the former chicken farmer's
sheer audacity and his contempt not only for the truth but for
the listening senators he must have known could see through
his deceptions and distortions. But he knew power-hungry
Republican senators—even the respectables of the Senate
club—would not expose him because *they didn't want to.*

McCarthy knew that some of his Republican colleagues—
even some Democrats who had deplored FDR and now opposed Truman and the Fair Deal—believed he was making
more effectively than anyone before him the "soft on communism" case against the Democrats and the administration;
they wanted to encourage, not deter, him. He believed the
inner club would never accept a roughneck like Joe McCarthy
or concede that its cherished rules and traditions could not
be imposed on a senator unwilling to conform to them.* Crucially, too, McCarthy understood that most senators were unwilling to risk being called unpatriotic or pro-communist.

On the Senate floor that February 20, Democratic leader
Scott Lucas of Illinois and other Democrats did challenge Mc-
Carthy, at least superficially—with Lucas trying to force him,
for instance, to confirm the figure he had used in Wheeling.

---

* He was wrong. The Senate's long-delayed condemnation of McCarthy in
1954 was in large part a rebuke for his unwillingness to play by its rules.

But with help from other Republicans, McCarthy refused to be pinned down. Party colleagues managed, in fact, to focus a confused debate on Truman's denial of loyalty files to Congress, and Lucas had, in effect, to forgo his demands.

The majority leader also agreed to Republican leader Kenneth Wherry's motion for a full-scale investigation of McCarthy's hoary charges—so far had the once-obscure Wisconsin senator forged upward from his thrown-together speech in Wheeling. Lucas even agreed, inexplicably, to a strange "compromise"—giving the proposed investigating committee power to subpoena administration loyalty files but not to probe specific charges made by McCarthy against specific persons. Perhaps the Democrats hoped to spare the Truman administration further embarrassment; but their agreement also precluded the possibility of exposing any distortions or falsehoods in McCarthy's speech. His low opinion of most of his colleagues must have been confirmed by this and other developments of February 20, 1950.

THE FOREIGN RELATIONS COMMITTEE was given jurisdiction over the proposed investigation, and Chairman Tom Connally, Democrat of Texas, loyally produced from beneath his ten-gallon hat a subcommittee apparently stacked against McCarthy. Its chairman was to be Millard Tydings of Maryland—not only an inner club member but one with whom McCarthy had already clashed in the Malmédy hearings. On the Republican side sat Henry Cabot Lodge of Massachusetts, a famous grandson who sometimes deserted his hereditary party; and Bourke B. Hickenlooper of Iowa, politically sympathetic to McCarthy but well known in the Senate for chronic ineptitude. With such friends, many thought, Joe McCarthy needed no enemies.

After the new Tydings subcommittee opened its hearings on March 8, 1950, however, McCarthy proceeded with the same buoyant self-confidence that he had shown on February 20. He often exhibited a psychological and intellectual superiority over those who sought to contain, restrain, or defeat him. And he demonstrated again his ability to defy the odds, an innate sense of how to turn adversity into profit.

Since Wheeling, he had been inundated with approving mail (often with money enclosed), media comment, and party support. This groundswell of backing surely intensified the self-confidence approaching arrogance that McCarthy had already demonstrated in the Malmédy hearings. He no longer had to pull on the sleeve of the likes of Tom Coleman or Bob Taft to get the attention and *regard* they had seldom shown him. These now poured down on Joe McCarthy from every direction, and he had become unrecognizable as the obscure judge playing cards for a living and willing to use courtroom recesses to drive anywhere to speak to anyone who would listen.

In four days of direct testimony to the Tydings panel, McCarthy boiled down his February 20 speech to nine cases. His appearances before the subcommittee were accompanied by screaming publicity from a press apparently infatuated

with the new star's shocking story of subversion and betrayal—at least with how he told it. But most of those he
named had only tenuous connections to the State Department, and all strongly rebuffed his charges—including two
familiar figures from earlier anticommunist scavenger hunts:
Harlow Shapley, the director of the Harvard College Ob-
servatory, and Frederick L. Schuman, a Williams College
professor.

McCarthy insisted that all those he named had at least a
connection—fuzzy and dubiously presented—to various
communist "front" groups. Even in the most prominent cases
he addressed—those of Owen Lattimore and Philip Jessup[17]—he suggested nothing more damning. Jessup at least
had a real relationship to the State Department as ambassador at large, but Lattimore's State Department connection
was less demonstrable. A Far East scholar and director of the
Page School of International Relations at Johns Hopkins University, Lattimore had served only as a State Department lec-
turer, consultant, and adviser, though he once had worked in
the Office of War Information.*

---

* Others in McCarthy's final nine were Dorothy Kenyon, a liberal New York
lawyer; Gustavo Duran, a former State Department and current UN employee; John Stewart Service, a U.S. diplomat; Haldore Hanson, an administrator in the State Department's Point 4 Program; and Esther Brunauer,
briefly a State Department employee, formerly of the American Association
of University Women.

Neither Republican nor Democratic senators on the Tydings panel attempted to conceal their partisanship, and several Republicans who were not members often visited the hearings to support their sometimes-beleaguered, always-outnumbered colleague. Democratic subcommittee members soon discovered that to deny McCarthy's accusations, it was necessary to repeat them, and that a dubious charge stated often enough circulated too quickly and too widely in an eager press to be refuted factually. Even Taft was quoted on the front page of the *New York Times* as having advised McCarthy, "If one case didn't work out, to bring up another."*

On March 21, perhaps exhilarated by the commotion he had caused and by his greater Senate acceptability, or maybe only by a good fight, McCarthy made his boldest charge: he loudly announced that he was ready to identify the No. 1 Soviet spy in the United States. No one had ever made such a dramatic promise; even if never justified, the charge would bring Joe McCarthy more prominence merely for his having made it—as he surely must have anticipated.

This new claim also caused Tydings to summon his subcommittee into a special session, demanding to hear the name of the top spy. McCarthy complied; but the identification he made behind closed subcommittee doors turned out

---

* March 23, 1950. Taft denied making the statement, but the apparently approving impact remained.

to be an anticlimax. In an executive session McCarthy declared the much-discussed scholar Owen Lattimore to be "definitely an espionage agent," though he disclosed no new evidence, or any evidence at all. He then boasted to the press, mentioning no names, that he had uncovered "the biggest espionage case" in U.S. history,[18] a charge heavily reported in headlines everywhere and perhaps as widely believed.

Congress being what it is, Lattimore's name was bound to "leak" from the executive session. In fact, with McCarthy's personal clearance, Drew Pearson in his national broadcast of March 26, 1950, disclosed that Lattimore was the person accused of being Moscow's top spy in America. Few events better illustrate the McCarthy-press collaboration that then existed.

Following the Lattimore flap, the New Hampshire Republican Styles Bridges—an éminence grise in his party personally committed to the anticommunist offensive against the Democrats and convinced of the State Department's betrayal of the Chinese nationalists—openly attacked Secretary of State Dean Acheson. Enraged, President Truman told a news conference that the Kremlin had no greater asset than efforts by the likes of Bridges, Wherry, and McCarthy to undercut U.S. foreign policy. McCarthy's inclusion in a presidential denunciation of Republican stars represented real status for a man who had been a Senate pariah only a few weeks earlier.

An unexpected new leader was suddenly standing side by side with the Old Guard and slugging it out with the president of the United States. With characteristic opportunism, McCarthy seized the leadership role Truman had incautiously handed him. In the Senate on March 30, 1950, he again slammed the Democrats and the administration for being soft on communists, zooming in on the State Department's Far East policy as a betrayal of nationalist China and repeating his Tydings subcommittee charges against Philip Jessup and John Stewart Service as treasonous culprits.

Predictably, however, he most strongly denounced Owen Lattimore—this time, in what should have been reported as a strategic retreat—not as Moscow's most valuable spy but as the architect of the State Department's subversive and pro-communist Far East policy. McCarthy also read to the Senate a letter he said Lattimore had written during World War II, showing—as McCarthy characterized it—Lattimore's communist leanings. But the Wisconsin senator refused to put what he said was a still-classified document into the *Congressional Record,* enhancing his accusation with the aura of secrecy.

McCarthy's speech that day was interrupted at one point by applause from the galleries, a rare and significant event in the austere Senate chamber. Despite the "stacked" Tydings subcommittee and his own failure to deliver anything like solid evidence of real subversion—much less Moscow's

No. 1 spy—McCarthy had blossomed into the Republicans' most famous spokesman on the anticommunist front. When Taft referred to him falsely but fulsomely as a "fighting Marine,"[19] an image sure to evoke admiration in 1950s America, the Wisconsin senator's political position was greatly enhanced and probably solidified. Whatever worries he might once have had about reelection in 1952 had become obsolete.

4

THE ATTITUDE OF A sizable number of Americans in early 1950 probably was voiced by Freda Utley, a chain-smoking, ash-scattering, apparently disillusioned ex-communist who had become a perennial *anti*communist witness. In her testimony to the Tydings subcommittee, she said:

"The Communist cancer must be cut out if we are to survive as a free nation. Perhaps in this operation *some healthy tissue on the fringe* will be destroyed" (italics added).

Much "healthy tissue" *was* destroyed in the Republican campaign to excise the supposed "cancer" of subversion from the Democratic Party and the Truman administration. In fact, by the time of Joe McCarthy's lunge into fame, such subversion as had once existed—substantial, apparently, particularly in the State and Treasury departments—had been largely eliminated by time, death, witnesses such as Whittaker

Chambers, Smith Act prosecutions,* and Truman's security measures.

A KGB memo dated March 1950—when McCarthy and the Tydings subcommittee were going round and round—lamented that "more than 40 most valuable agents" in the United States had been exposed and were "impossible to replace." With the Soviet Union no longer a wartime ally and the U.S. Communist Party driven underground and unable to act as the effective liaison with the KGB that it once had been, even dedicated leftists were no longer willing to become spies for Moscow. An American perception that the U.S. government was "awash in treachery" nevertheless remained. Because of this perception, fed by Republican charges, McCarthy could and did flourish, though in Ted Morgan's phrase, he had only "arrived on the battlefield after the battle was over to finish off the wounded."[20]

Utley, for example, gave McCarthy little help; she denied to the subcommittee that Owen Lattimore was a spy and offered no evidence that he was even a communist. The Tydings hearings devoted to Lattimore, in fact, were mostly a bust.

A parade of witnesses, including former Communist Party chairman Earl Browder, denied that Lattimore was a

* The Alien Registration Act of 1940, frequently amended and named for Representative Howard Smith (D-VA), made it unlawful to advocate or teach the overthrow of the U.S. government or to belong to any group pursuing that end.

communist. Chairman Tydings announced, moreover, that four members of the seven-man subcommittee—necessarily including Lodge or Hickenlooper or both—had seen Lattimore's loyalty file* and had found nothing in it to suggest that he was or had been a communist. The file must have been "raped," McCarthy declared, with customary assurance and lack of proof.

Even McCarthy's much-ballyhooed star witness, Louis Budenz, failed to make the case that Lattimore was a spy, though Budenz insisted that Lattimore in various unspecified ways was under Moscow's control. A former managing editor of the *Daily Worker,* Budenz had joined the Communist Party in 1935, stayed with it through the Moscow show trials and the brief Soviet alliance with Hitler, but defected in 1945 to reenter the Roman Catholic Church and to become, like Freda Utley, an oft-called witness in the anticommunist cause.

Budenz's subcommittee testimony was undermined by his own history: in the countless hours he had been grilled by the FBI between 1946 and 1950 and in his frequent testimony before courts and committees, he had never accused Owen Lattimore. Worse, he had told a State Department security officer in 1947 that he knew nothing to indicate that Lattimore was a party member. Budenz's credibility was further

---

* Made grudgingly available by the Truman administration but only to the subcommittee.

weakened when the subcommittee discovered that he had conferred—*before* testifying—with its Republican counsel, McCarthy's ally Robert Morris.

The executive session, however, gave McCarthy another opportunity to use the press when he disclosed what Budenz supposedly had testified. McCarthy was not a member of the Tydings subcommittee and had been excluded from that particular closed session; but no reporter asked him how he knew what had been said, whether he was reporting it accurately, or what right he had to share testimony from an executive session.

Only slightly less irresponsible was the performance of two stars of the *New York Times*. Arthur Krock, the conservative columnist, commented that "many fair-minded persons" were beginning to change their opinions about McCarthy's allegations. This was hardly objective reporting since it gave the false impression that Budenz had validated McCarthy's charges. William S. White, the "dean" of Senate reporters, merely parroted Budenz's uncorroborated testimony that he had been "officially informed" that Lattimore was a communist. By whom? Budenz never said. And were the words of either Budenz or the "official" informer corroborated in any manner? Bill White did not say.[21]

In fact, Budenz's most startling charge was not against Lattimore at all; instead, in an executive session he alleged that Haldore Hanson was a Communist Party member. An excited Joe McCarthy bolted from the executive session to tell

the waiting press that Budenz had named a high State Department official as a CP member. Three days later on the
Senate floor, McCarthy personally "outed" Hanson as the alleged State Department communist fingered by Budenz.

When the hearings came to a close in the glare of
McCarthy-generated headlines, Republicans and anti-Truman
Democrats appeared to be winning something like the game
Hitler had played in Germany. Even insubstantial charges
were never quite disposed of by denials, which themselves
called attention to the accusations. The constant allegations
that the Democrats and the Truman administration had been
subverted from abroad and infiltrated at home suggested that
smoke must be hovering over *some* hidden administration fire.

The more the president and his supporters responded, the
more frantic and shrill they seemed—particularly to those
disposed anyway to see communists, traitors, dupes, "parlor
pinks and parlor punks" (McCarthy's phrase) as the cause of
everything from the Soviet A-bomb to the flight of the Chinese nationalists to the invasion of South Korea in June 1950.

Even Owen Lattimore's angry testimony on April 6 that
McCarthy's allegations were outright lies did little good because of Lattimore's obvious contempt for the subcommittee
and for the charges against him.

NEVERTHELESS, BY ANY objective standard, McCarthy had
struck out. He had produced no evidence that Owen Lattimore was the major Soviet spy in the United States or a spy

at all, or even the architect of a treasonous Far East policy—
and only dubious assertions that Lattimore actually was a
communist. Yet, as after the earlier hearings that did not factually support him, McCarthy emerged with greater public
and party support. He showed no awareness of, certainly no
remorse for, what many called his questionable tactics. Mc-
Carthy's followers in the Senate and elsewhere had rallied
round as if he had been revealed as a prophet. Why?

One explanation lies in the growing menace of the Cold
War, the Soviet explosion of an A-bomb, the spy scandals in
Canada and Britain plus the *Hiss* case in the United States,
the so-called loss of China, the sudden Korean War, and the
Republican smearing of the Truman administration. What
Woodrow Wilson had called "the atmosphere of events" led
all too many nervous Americans to consider subversion in
Washington plausible, cover-up likely, and Joe McCarthy a
bold patriot exposing subversion's soft spots.

A second explanation, however, lies in McCarthy's performance*—the drama and boldness of his charges, his stubborn repetition of them, his refusal to back down, and his
apparent willingness to take on anyone, from the president to
obscure editorial writers. Even the thinness of his evidence
and the dubious credibility of his witnesses made him seem,
to some Americans, willing to take large personal and politi-

---

* Had it been in a Hollywood movie, it was of Oscar caliber.

cal risks in his justified wrath at communists and fellow travelers, his determination to "root out" what he insisted was treason in high places. "Risk taking" in America, from Evel Knievel to Warren Buffett, is almost always admired—and Joe McCarthy had become a master at appearing to battle the odds.

Then and later in his career, McCarthy was much like a juggler, always in danger of dropping one or more of the numerous balls he had in the air, but somehow sustaining his act. Always, too, in the early years of his notoriety, he had the aid of a press that prided itself on more courage and skepticism than it usually displayed.

Once, for an egregious example, the now-defunct *Washington Star* quoted the senator quoting a former Office of Strategic Services (OSS) officer, one Frank Bielaski, to the effect that "the secrets of the atomic bomb" had been transmitted to Moscow "six months before . . . Hiroshima." When the story appeared, Bielaski was still testifying to the Tydings subcommittee. Even when his testimony was complete, he had said nothing of the kind. McCarthy, with the help of an acquiescent newspaper, had made sure his wishful version of Bielaski's statement would be published even before Bielaski had had the chance to say it.[22]

McCarthy's name in the headlines—charging this or claiming that; making accusations sometimes plausible, more often outrageous—kept him in the public eye, enjoying and stimulating the kind of glory he had craved since his chicken-farming days. It was not, however, undiluted glory.

THE OPPOSITION McCARTHY aroused from the start was real and highly charged. As the two national parties wrangled more often over patriotism than policy, as traditional "values" were claimed and flouted—with "Americanism" asserted and disputed—millions of Americans saw greater subversion of their own and their country's ideals in McCarthy's unsupported Red-scare accusations than in whatever foreign influence there might have been in Washington.

Across the nation, millions feared and denounced Joe McCarthy and his technique of "smearing" opponents with charges of distorted or fictitious misdeeds. Herblock, the great *Washington Post* editorial-page artist, labeled this technique "McCarthyism." As a malediction, the phrase entered the language and even some dictionaries; it has survived its progenitor (often drawn by Herblock as a bearded thug emerging from a sewer). "McCarthyism" remains an epithet for almost any disreputable tactic, particularly smearing opponents.

To McCarthy's ardent backers, the powerful and emotional opposition he aroused—from liberals, leftists, Senate traditionalists, Truman Democrats, some Republicans, and the president himself—supported their belief that, at last, a patriotic and fearless American was making the dangerous fight against the hidden influences that were taking the nation down the wrong road. As the Cold War continued and a hot war flared in Korea, Joe McCarthy—passionately admired, passionately hated—became a more notable figure than he ever could have dreamed of in his Marquette classes or his Appleton courtroom or even while posing beside warplanes on Guadalcanal.

With his command of drama and deception, his reckless intuition, and his thirst for distinction, he had shrewdly exploited the dark places of the American psyche. But even in one of the most frightening periods of the Cold War and even with the aid of the press, Joe McCarthy never truly seized national leadership.

MILLARD TYDINGS'S SUBCOMMITTEE published a vitriolic report denouncing McCarthy's February 20 charges as "a fraud and a hoax" and lambasting him personally for putting forth deliberate falsehoods. Unabashed, the senator quickly responded that Tydings's report gave "a green light to the Red fifth column." William Jenner, Republican of Indiana and a staunch McCarthy supporter, called the report the "most scandalous and brazen whitewash of treasonable conspiracy in our history." Homer Ferguson, Republican of Michigan, charged that the subcommittee report had combined "the techniques of Goebbels and Vishinsky."

Nevertheless, the Senate approved the report in a straight party-line vote—Democrats for, Republicans against—thus

further identifying Republicans* with the hunt for subversion
and disloyalty in the government. The Democratic leadership
had forced itself into the awkward position of being partisan
defenders of a supposedly Red-riddled party, State Department, and administration.

That summer of 1950 an omnibus internal security bill,
the so-called McCarran Act (the life-crowning work of the
conservative Democrat Pat McCarran of Nevada) came before
the Senate. McCarran wielded formidable power through his
chairmanship of the Judiciary Committee, hence influence on
judicial appointments; but opponents of his security measure
argued accurately that it endangered civil liberties.

A number of Democratic liberals put together a substitute—one that reflected, unfortunately, their fear of being accused of sympathy for domestic communism. The substitute
provided for the internment of suspected subversives (a "con-
centration camp bill," a Truman aide called it) if the president
declared an internal security emergency. In the parliamentary
snarl that developed, this oddity was *added to* rather than sub-
stituted for the McCarran Act, with the ludicrous result that
many Democratic liberals, including Hubert Humphrey, Paul
Douglas, William Benton, and Clinton Anderson, found them-

---

* Notable party dissenters included governors James Duff of Pennsylvania,
Alfred Driscoll of New Jersey, and Earl Warren of California.

selves voting for McCarran's bill—which passed, seventy to seven, with the Democratic leadership folding abjectly.

Some liberals then urged Truman to veto the very act they had voted to approve. Courageously, he did. Predictably, both houses of Congress overrode the veto—but not before Humphrey and William Langer of North Dakota staged a futile last-ditch filibuster. Langer, a maverick known as "Wild Bill" and the single Republican senator in opposition, called the McCarran Act "one of the most vicious . . . dangerous pieces of legislation against the people" ever proposed.

Though he was not a leading player in this tragicomedy, Joe McCarthy benefited immensely—because the quick override was a graphic public indicator of where power lay in Washington. And the clear meaning of the McCarran Act's mostly untroubled passage was that neither the White House nor Congress offered a reliable levee against the rising tide of anticommunism—which more and more seemed synonymous with McCarthyism.

ACROSS THE NATION in the 1950 elections, McCarthyism was a popular, if disputed, political tactic. The fame and the stinging rhetoric of its primary practitioner—who did not have to campaign for his own seat that year—made Joe McCarthy a natural Republican leader. No longer the little-known and mostly disliked politician his party had sent on a second-rate speaking tour less than a year earlier, the Wisconsin senator was in hot demand and responded with more than thirty speeches in fifteen states. His message was the same everywhere: Hunt down the Reds and get rid of the "com-miecrats" in government.

By then, profiting from his Marquette public-speaking courses or exploiting his speechwriters, McCarthy had become a daunting phrase maker—denouncing some opponents, for instance, as "egg-sucking phony liberals" who indulged in "pitiful whining." Others were "prancing mimics of the Moscow party line" or "danced to the Moscow tune." Tydings had conducted "Operation Whitewash." Special scorn, of course, was reserved for Secretary of State Dean Acheson and for aides such as Philip Jessup: "dilettante diplomats" who "whined" and "whimpered" and "cringed" before the communists.

Nineteen fifty was a year of high hopes for the Republican Party. Officials of the New Deal and the Fair Deal had been in office for nearly twenty controversial years—too long in any election. Harry Truman's approval rating was down, at one point as low as 26 percent. His old association with the Kansas City political machine as well as alleged relationships with so-called five-percenters* damaged him, as did the lingering traces of both the Henry Wallace and the Dixiecrat revolts of 1948.

---

* Influence wielders accused of accepting 5-percent rake-offs.

The South was no longer reliably Democratic (though its big switch to the GOP was yet to come), the big city bosses had been weakened, labor's postwar strikes had provoked heavy criticism, and Truman's fiery campaign style was less effective when he was supporting candidates other than himself. The Korean War, after its first weeks, was a Democratic liability, and Republicans continued in their loud insistence that both the administration and the Democratic Party had been infiltrated by communists. A common theme that year was that a Red-influenced Acheson had "invited" North Korea to invade South Korea by excluding the latter in a public statement from a largely imaginary U.S. "defense perimeter" in Asia.

McCarthy's personal campaign focus was against Millard Tydings of Maryland, as was only to be expected after their harsh joustings in the subcommittee hearings. Tydings was running for a fifth term, a rarity in almost any state. Though a power in the Senate and a member of its inner club, he was in fact vulnerable—a Democrat in what was to be a mostly Republican year, in a state not deaf to the disturbing echoes of fighting in Korea. Well known as a conservative, Tydings had voted consistently against social legislation and civil rights measures, thus alienating labor and offending blacks (a significant segment of Baltimore voters). The Maryland Democratic vote had been declining for years, the party organization was riven over a state sales tax, and Governor Preston

Lane was on the way to defeat by the popular Republican mayor of Baltimore, Theodore McKeldin.

Such on-paper vulnerability was not enough for McCarthy. He ignored any suggestion that it might be unseemly for a senator from one state to campaign against a senator from another (they were, after all, of different parties) and made three appearances in Maryland. Each time he accused Tydings of "protecting communists" and shielding traitors. Two of Tydings's Democratic primary opponents took up McCarthy's charge that the incumbent had whitewashed Red influence in the Truman administration. By Election Day in November, this issue had been thoroughly aired throughout Maryland.

According to a later Senate investigation of the Maryland election, McCarthy's personal appearances were less than half of his real contribution to the campaign against Tydings. McCarthy used his national status to raise big money for John Marshall Butler, Tydings's undistinguished opponent; Butler was able to outspend Tydings, three to one. McCarthy helped plan Butler's strategy, and McCarthy and his staff (including his future wife, Jean Kerr) largely controlled Butler's campaign. With the help of Ruth McCormick Miller, editor of the *Washington Times-Herald* (a property of her uncle, Colonel Robert McCormick of the *Chicago Tribune*), they imported a Chicago public relations man to manage Butler's day-by-day campaigning and to bear down on the whitewash charge.

Miller's newspaper, circulated heavily in Baltimore and Washington suburbs, backed Butler in news and editorial columns and provided cut-rate printing. McCarthy aides even resurrected his old postcard gimmick.

The McCarthy group, though not necessarily the senator, had the heaviest hand in publishing a tabloid newspaper that exaggerated all charges against Tydings. Most famously, it featured a photo doctored to show Tydings in cordial conversation with Earl Browder, chairman of the Communist Party.*

McCarthy's long-ago Tenth District victory over Judge Werner foreshadowed the Maryland result: to the surprise of the general public but not to Maryland political buffs, Tydings lost by more than forty thousand votes. What FDR's attempted "purge" of Tydings could not do in 1938, Joe McCarthy— whose intervention in Maryland was no secret—seemingly had done in 1950.[23] McCarthy—whether one approved of him or not—appeared able to go into action anywhere else and defeat any other politician at whom he had cause to take aim.

That year Democratic majority leader Scott Lucas, another McCarthy critic, was defeated in Illinois. Representative Richard Nixon, another famous Red hunter, was elected to the Senate in California, defeating the liberal Democrat

---

* Even McCarthy's political benefactor, "Boss" Tom Coleman of Wisconsin, disassociated himself from the use of the "composite" photo.

Helen Gahagan Douglas. In a Democratic primary in North
Carolina, another liberal, Senator Frank P. Graham, was
ousted by Willis Smith in a McCarthy-tinged campaign partly
steered by Jesse Helms (a local radio commentator who would
be elected to the Senate himself in 1972).

The obvious lesson for politicians: Don't give McCarthy
cause to take aim.

BOTH THE LESSON and the assumption behind it were exaggerated. McCarthy's prime victim, Millard Tydings, given his
basic political weaknesses in Maryland, could have been defeated by a strong opponent even if McCarthy had stayed out
of the campaign. And McCarthy was not that powerful a
kingmaker; even with his help—doctored photo and all—
John Marshall Butler ran far behind the state's other Republican winner, Theodore McKeldin.

As for Scott Lucas, he lost his seat in Illinois not to Joe
McCarthy but to Everett Dirksen, a well-known House member renowned as "the wizard of ooze" for his fulsome oratory.
Campaigning hard since early 1949, Dirksen—like Butler—
hammered home the Republican issue of communists in government and was helped by rising discontent about the war
in Korea. As important was a weak Democratic candidate for
sheriff of Cook County (Chicago), a target of criminal investigation and many hostile headlines. A huge downstate vote,
not offset this time by the usual Democratic landslide in
Chicago, carried Dirksen into the Senate.

In California the Republican candidate also benefited from factors other than McCarthyism. McCarthy appeared uninvited to speak in Los Angeles, declaring that "the chips are down . . . between the American people and the administration commiecrat party of betrayal." Nixon engaged in plenty of Red-scare rhetoric, labeling Douglas "the pink lady." But Douglas might well have lost a statewide race anyway, owing to a divisive Democratic Party primary, the *Los Angeles Times'* energetic support for Nixon, Murray Chotiner's astute management of the Nixon campaign, and the pink lady's inept tactics. Douglas did not have much support from Washington; neither Harry Truman nor Speaker Sam Rayburn liked her, and Nixon's House colleague John F. Kennedy of Massachusetts contributed to the ample Nixon treasury ten years before the two competed for the presidency.

McCarthy failed flatly to cause the defeat of Senator Brien McMahon of Connecticut, a member of the Democratic majority of the Tydings subcommittee. ("Lucas provided the whitewash," McCarthy observed. "McMahon brought the brush, Tydings the bucket.") As in Maryland, McCarthy appeared and spoke three times, but McMahon had no strong opponent and faced no Chicago-style scandal; his Irish Catholic religion and ancestry placed him in the mainstream of his state's strong Democratic Party. On election night he led the balloting—McCarthy or no McCarthy.

In North Carolina Smith's primary victory over Frank Graham was due more to thinly veiled racism than to anti-Red accusations, although Graham had many times been a target of the latter. In a more openly McCarthyite campaign, George Smathers defeated Senator Claude Pepper in the Florida Democratic primary, after calling him "Red Pepper" and allegedly accusing him of "nepotism with his sister."

Overall, despite McCarthy's efforts, popularity, and many imitators, Republicans still failed to realize their hopes of recapturing the control of Congress that had been lost in 1948 to Truman's "Give 'em hell" campaign. The president came out fighting again, claiming that Republicans who harped on the Red issue had "lost . . . all sense of restraint, all sense of patriotic decency." The Republicans did, however, gain twenty-eight seats in the House and five in the Senate, maintaining the tradition that the party in the White House loses seats in a midterm election. The GOP was positioned nicely for the 1952 election. (In Ohio Robert Taft, then considered the party's likely presidential nominee, easily won reelection without help from Joe McCarthy.)

If McCarthy's political power was somewhat overstated after 1950, that power nevertheless seemed real. Not many people had the time or the means to study the political situation in Maryland in 1950 or to analyze McCarthy's failure in Connecticut. If a political fixture such as Millard Tydings could go down after incurring McCarthy's wrath, it appeared that anyone could.

On May 24, 1951, Wisconsin's junior senator—clearly feeling if not exaggerating his power—took the Senate floor to launch one of his most venomous attacks on a familiar target: Secretary of State Dean Acheson. "You and your criminal crowd betrayed us," McCarthy declaimed in his monotone. "You should not only resign . . . but you should remove yourself from this country and go to the nation for which you have been struggling . . . so long."

Despite these incendiary remarks about one of their own, Democratic senators appeared to be too intimidated to give Acheson more than "minimal defense."[24]

MILLARD TYDINGS DID NOT challenge the outcome of the Maryland election, but he urged the Senate, in writing, to inquire into what he called with considerable accuracy a "scandalous, scurrilous, libelous and unlawful" campaign. In February 1951 a subcommittee of the Committee on Rules undertook an investigation and scheduled public hearings. Shrewdly, McCarthy declined to testify; but numerous witnesses did, and the panel was able to document serious financial irregularities in Butler's campaign. Ultimately, in spite of the generally fearful Senate attitude, the subcommittee issued a report highly critical of Senator McCarthy.

His prompt response was predictable—the subcommittee had been willing to "ignore or whitewash communist influences in our government." The full Rules Committee nevertheless approved the subcommittee report, nine to three. McCarthy, by then a member of the committee, of course voted with the minority. Two Republicans, Margaret Smith of

Maine and Robert Hendrickson of New Jersey,* joined the
Democrats in the majority, making the Maryland report "bipartisan." But the panel made no recommendations, and
nothing came of its work.

Nothing, that is, until its report caught the eye of Senator William Benton of Connecticut, a Democrat appointed to
succeed McCarthy's early antagonist, Raymond Baldwin, who
had resigned to accept a state judgeship. Benton had been
elected to serve the last two years of Baldwin's term. Formerly
a partner in the advertising agency Benton & Bowles, Benton
had been board chairman of the *Encyclopaedia Britannica*
and an assistant secretary of state in the Truman administration. The last of these positions should have given him reason to beware of Joe McCarthy, but Benton apparently shared
other senators' personal distaste for their Wisconsin colleague
rather than the political timidity that caused many of them to
look the other way. Benton put forward a resolution requiring
the Senate to determine whether or not Joseph R. McCarthy
should be expelled.

The chamber was mostly appalled. Benton had no chance
of winning the two-thirds vote his resolution required. He
knew it but wished to revive the Maryland report and perhaps
help defeat McCarthy in Wisconsin in 1952.[25] Probably he

---

* Hendrickson and Smith had joined in a "declaration of conscience" against
McCarthy on June 1, 1950.

should have been less aggressive; he had little influence among colleagues, who regarded him as an "amateur" and his resolution as hasty and indiscreet. And the fact was that numerous senators were afraid to challenge McCarthy, who promptly called Benton "the hero of every Communist and crook in and out of government." Benton's resolution was quickly referred to the same subcommittee that had probed the Maryland election, where it was expected to be forgotten.

Indeed, it might have been ignored had McCarthy not recklessly offended Ernest McFarland of Arizona, Lucas's successor as majority leader. McFarland took umbrage at a speech denouncing twenty-six former and present State Department officials, a speech in which McCarthy also attacked the Maryland subcommittee and one of its members, Thomas Hennings of Missouri. Urged on by McFarland, the panel decided almost in self-defense to hear Benton and to deny McCarthy the power of cross-examination.

Given this opportunity, Benton boldly tore into McCarthy for deceit, fraud, fabrication, and more—even bringing up the old Lustron fee controversy—but focused especially on his contention that the Wisconsin senator had brought the Senate into disrepute. McCarthy counterattacked continuously and deftly, not only with his usual outcry about whitewash and communist influence but also subverting subcommittee staff members and obfuscating the issues involved.

One example was a press statement by Daniel G. Buckley, a former assistant counsel to the subcommittee, who claimed falsely to have been "summarily dismissed" from its "insidious campaign to destroy any man who fights communist subversion"—obviously meaning Joe McCarthy. The statement may have been prepared by McCarthy aides who had been in touch with Buckley; he later was hired by the Republican National Committee.

The controversy caused by Benton, the hearings, and McCarthy's visceral reaction reached a climax in April 1952 in a second resolution, put forward by Rules Committee chairman Carl Hayden, to discharge the subcommittee of responsibility for the Benton resolution. Hayden was trying to clear the air, but his move was defeated by the Senate, sixty to zero. This did not signal whether the Senate wanted to close or to continue the McCarthy investigation because McCarthy had so dexterously clouded the question of what was being voted upon—confidence in him or in the subcommittee?—that no one was sure what he was voting for, and no one could tell who was for or against or merely neutral about Joe McCarthy. That, indeed, was the way the Senate wanted things in 1951.

The subcommittee considering the Benton resolution continued its work without much enthusiasm, conducting four days of public hearings during which McCarthy was heavily criticized—but only for the conflict of interest involved in the old Lustron deal. The outlines of that ambiguous transaction had been so long known that little damage was done to McCarthy—and even less to McCarthyism—by the subcommittee.

The tables were turned on William Benton when McCarthy introduced a counterresolution calling for an investigation of Benton's State Department service and threatening to disclose Benton's income-tax records. So numerous were the distractions, including suit and countersuit, and so effective were McCarthy's defensive maneuvers, that it was not until January 2, 1952—the last day of an expiring Congress—that the so-called Hennings Report (Thomas Hennings had become subcommittee chairman) finally was issued.

The report was barely bipartisan, Republican Hendrickson of New Jersey having signed it despite McCarthy's pressure on him not to do so. But the document largely ignored the many political and social issues raised by McCarthyism and the "Reds in government" campaign. Instead, the Hennings Report focused narrowly on the Lustron issue and other aspects of McCarthy's finances. Crucially, it did devote several pages to an account of how the senator had frustrated and thwarted the Benton investigation. In effect, McCarthy's importance in national and international affairs was passed over as if it did not exist; instead, his affronts to the U.S. Senate were emphasized, with the report concluding that the junior senator from Wisconsin had displayed "disdain and contempt for the rules and wishes" of those he was supposed to respect. There were no recommendations for action of any kind.

Two years later, in 1954, in a different time and atmosphere, the Hennings Report became a published bestseller. Its frank description of Joe McCarthy's attitude toward the Senate and his colleagues would come back to haunt him— as would his sixty thousand–word, three-hour speech in the Senate on June 14, 1951, attacking General George C. Marshall.

5

GEORGE MARSHALL WAS Truman's secretary of defense, formerly his secretary of state and special envoy to China, and a five-star general widely revered for his high character and overall leadership of American forces during World War II. Despite his desire to command the invasion of Europe in 1944, General Marshall had allowed his protégé, Dwight D. Eisenhower, to have the post. No one, save Franklin Roosevelt and Harry Truman, had done more than Marshall to benefit Eisenhower—who in June 1951 was considered a major, if unannounced, candidate for the presidency in 1952.

McCarthy's unwise attack on the iconic Marshall may have been prompted by Marshall's admission that he had counseled Truman to fire General Douglas MacArthur—another great military hero but one who had flaunted his disagreements with Truman, the commander in chief of the U.S. Armed Forces, on the conduct of the Korean War. Marshall considered such insubordination as virtually sacrilege; but the president's dismissal of MacArthur on April 11, 1951, briefly outraged the nation, particularly Republicans who claimed that Truman was "soft on communism." While talking to reporters in Milwaukee about Truman's decision, McCarthy said—he thought privately—that "the son of a bitch should be impeached." He suggested also that the president had been drinking when he fired MacArthur[26]—surely the pot calling the kettle black. When these words inevitably appeared in print, many Americans—no matter what their views of MacArthur, Truman, or McCarthy—were shocked to hear their president referred to as a drunken son of a bitch.

McCarthy and others had criticized Marshall before Truman fired MacArthur, mostly for Marshall's supposed role in "losing China" to communism; that accusation was indeed a main theme of McCarthy's June 14 speech. But few criticisms had equaled McCarthy's savage philippic—which included the assertion that General Marshall had been part of "a conspiracy of infamy so black that, when it is finally exposed, its principals shall be forever deserving of the maledictions of all honest men."*

This outburst—much of which does not appear to have been composed by McCarthy himself and the bulk of which

---

* Before delivering the speech on the Senate floor, McCarthy had publicly promised to expose "a conspiracy so immense and an infamy so black as to dwarf any previous such venture in the history of man." *New York Times,* June 13, 1951, p. 12. This advance publicity caused most Democrats to boycott the Senate chamber when McCarthy rose to speak.

had to be inserted into the *Congressional Record* owing to its length—disturbed even some of McCarthy's sycophants. Needless to say, no trace of this enormous conspiracy—or any other involving George Marshall—has ever been discovered. Unless a shrewd politician was deluded enough to think that the nation's eruption over MacArthur's firing would harden into permanent opposition to Marshall and Truman, McCarthy's motivation for making such a foolhardy speech is far from clear. Did McCarthy consider it a cynical part of a cynical but successful anticommunist campaign, or did he believe what he was saying about Marshall? If so, he must have believed in most of his anticommunist pronouncements.

For the time being—perhaps to his own wonderment and probably to his growing vanity—Joseph R. McCarthy was indisputably a power in the land. But as the nation moved toward another presidential election year, the one-time pariah from Wisconsin had sown seeds of resistance—not least in the bizarre Marshall speech—that would sprout and grow beyond his or perhaps anyone's imaginings.

EARLY IN 1952 a conventional Republican contest for the presidential nomination exploded into a confrontation over the long-simmering differences between the conservative isolationist and moderate internationalist wings of the party—the former represented by Taft of Ohio, the most admired Republican in the Senate; the latter by the enormously popular Eisenhower. President Truman had sent "Ike," as he was almost universally known to Americans, back to Europe as the first commander of NATO forces. Better casting for the show-down could hardly have been imagined.

Eisenhower was a military hero from the "good war" against Hitler and Hirohito; in 1952 he was sought by both parties as a presidential candidate. He finally let it be known that, though unregistered, he was a lifelong Republican. Taft had been an active candidate in 1948, losing to Governor Thomas Dewey of New York; the favorite of orthodox Republicans, he had piled up a lead of about 40 percent of the delegates who would choose the 1952 nominee at the Chicago convention. Eisenhower was implored to run by such moderates as Senator Lodge of Massachusetts, Governor Duff of Pennsylvania, Dewey, and Herbert Brownell, a New York Republican who had managed the Dewey campaign in 1948. When Eisenhower abandoned the ambiguous attitude toward the presidential nomination that he had maintained since World War II* and announced that he would run against Taft, a knockdown, drag-out intraparty battle became inevitable.

In a write-in campaign in the New Hampshire primary, Eisenhower had already defeated Taft; he had also polled more than a hundred thousand votes in another write-in campaign

---

* It's still not certain whether Eisenhower actually was playing a "hard to get" game. By late 1951 and early 1952, he appears definitely to have been angling for the nomination.

in Minnesota, against that state's "favorite son," Governor Harold Stassen. As an active candidate, Eisenhower proved effective though inexperienced. Until the convention opened, however, Taft dominated nonprimary Republican states and party organizations and managed to maintain his lead. By the time the candidates and their backers entered a bitter convention at Chicago, their competition had become personal as well as ideological. Taft boasted 530 delegates to Eisenhower's 427, according to a contemporary Associated Press estimate.

Eisenhower abhorred Joe McCarthy because of his attacks on Marshall and because of McCarthy's "coarse familiarity."* But as the favorite of most party leaders, Taft controlled convention organization and the lineup of speakers; he scheduled McCarthy for an evening speech, though the senator had officially stayed out of the Taft-Eisenhower conflict and instead endorsed General MacArthur—a once-likely candidate who had "just faded away" after Truman sacked him in 1951.

McCARTHY HAD ALREADY done his characteristic bit for the Republican Party. That spring at Chicago's Stevens Hotel, he said in a news conference that he had "documentation" to prove that on a specific day earlier in 1952, Adlai Stevenson—then the governor of Illinois and a possible Democratic

---

* Richard Nixon's description in his memoir *RN* (New York: Grosset & Dunlap, 1978).

presidential candidate—had participated in a "secret meeting right here in Chicago with members of the Communist Party."

Most of the press rushed away to print the sensational story, but Robert Schulman of *Time* magazine, who had no deadline pressure, approached McCarthy and asked for the documentation.

"Get this guy's name and arrange for him to get what he wants," the senator instructed an aide—who then told Schulman to send a written request to McCarthy's Washington office. Suspicious, Schulman returned to the Time-Life bureau, called Governor Stevenson's office, and was given detailed corroboration that on the day of the supposed "secret meeting" with communists in Chicago, Adlai Stevenson had been in London. After Schulman telephoned this information to the Time bureau in New York, he hung up to find a visitor inquiring if there were any messages for her.

"I'm Clare Luce," she said. More than fifty years later, Schulman remembered "the startlingly white, alabaster look" of Mrs. Henry Luce's hands. He told her about McCarthy's false charge and she replied bluntly:

"McCarthy is a charlatan. . . . [H]e has taken advantage of the void left by more responsible critics of the Stalinist threat."*

---

* Private correspondence with Robert Schulman, now a retired columnist for the *Louisville Courier-Journal*. *Time* magazine did not publish his refutation of McCarthy's charge.

When Eisenhower arrived in Chicago for the Republican convention only a few months later, he was displeased to discover that McCarthy was listed for a major address. But he could do nothing about it, and McCarthy was duly introduced to the convention and its national television audience as "an able and patriotic" senator and "that fighting Marine from Wisconsin." He had reached a political apex denied to many perhaps more deserving persons. But Tailgunner Joe's boilerplate speech, like General MacArthur's keynote message, while enthusiastically received was quickly forgotten; neither appeared to make a difference in the surprisingly quick outcome of the convention. Owing mostly to a ploy developed by the crafty Brownell—and ironically known as the "fair play amendment"*—Eisenhower eked out a hard-fought victory on the first ballot, after Stassen, sensing the trend, had swung his delegates to the general.

The victory was very nearly Pyrrhic because, in one of the last truly contested conventions before the parties allowed these great gatherings to be choreographed by and for television, the Republicans were riven almost down the middle. The internationalist nominee paid a high price for his narrow victory, accepting a platform with isolationist planks that denounced Truman's containment policy, promised the "liberation" of Eastern Europe, condemned the Yalta agreements,

---

* Brownell's plan resulted in seating Eisenhower delegates in place of challenged Taft delegates from several states.

and specifically charged that the Democrats had "shielded traitors" in the government. As a further sop to the Republican Old Guard and an added appeal to rabid anticommunists, Eisenhower allowed party leaders to choose Richard Nixon as his running mate.

After surviving early campaign "slush fund" charges, Nixon rewarded his selection with slashing attacks on a "spineless" Truman and on the Democratic nominee—Adlai "the Appeaser" Stevenson, with his "Ph.D. from Dean Acheson's Cowardly College of Communist Containment." Nixon visited Wisconsin to support his "good friend" Joe McCarthy* and said publicly that he and Eisenhower would back all Republican Senate and House nominees. Asked about that promise by reporters, Eisenhower swallowed hard but agreed to back McCarthy as a Republican—then added pointedly: "I am not going to campaign for or give blanket endorsement to any man who does anything that I believe to be un-American in its methods and procedures."

Eisenhower seemed unaware that the two statements virtually contradicted each other but, in a speech at Denver, made his position somewhat clearer by defending George Marshall as a patriot and a "man of real selflessness." Eisen-

---

* McCarthy hardly needed Nixon's help for reelection, despite a Democratic charge that he was "a tax-dodging, character-assassinating, racetrack-gambling, complete and contemptible liar."

hower insisted he had "no patience with anyone who can find in [Marshall's] record of service for this country anything to criticize." How, then, voters might have wondered, could he support the man who had made the "vast conspiracy" speech of June 1951?

MCCARTHY SCORED a huge renomination victory in Wisconsin in the Republican primary on September 9, 1952; a nervous Eisenhower campaign staff thereafter insisted that the reluctant general had little choice but to make a swing through the state.

As if to compensate for this necessity, the nominee had one of his speech writers, Emmet John Hughes, insert the following words in the draft of a speech scheduled for October 3 in Milwaukee:

> Let me be quite specific. I know that charges of disloyalty have, in the past, been leveled against General George C. Marshall. I have been privileged for thirty-five years to know General Marshall personally. I know him, as a man and a soldier, to be dedicated with singular selflessness and the profoundest patriotism to the service of America.

Hughes's paragraph concluded that "this episode," plainly meaning McCarthy's attack on Marshall, "is a sobering lesson in the way freedom must not defend itself."

On the Eisenhower campaign train, some aides maintained that the rebuff to McCarthy, if delivered in his home state, would damage the entire Wisconsin ticket. News of the debate caused by the proposed statement got back to McCarthy's home ground, where Republican leaders were already worried by reports that Eisenhower might ultimately refuse to appear in Wisconsin.

Their concern may have been fed when Eisenhower, in another obligatory campaign appearance in Indiana, endorsed Indiana's Republican ticket without mentioning McCarthy's ally, Senator William Jenner. Jenner was on the platform and, at the end of the speech, leaped to his feet to embrace a startled, obviously displeased Eisenhower—a scene copiously photographed and one that immediately caused the vice chairman of the national Young Republican Club to switch his support to Adlai Stevenson.[27]

As Eisenhower's campaign train reached Peoria, Illinois, on October 2, 1952, Wisconsin Republican committeeman Henry Ringling, Governor Walter Kohler, and Senator Joseph R. McCarthy arrived to pin down Ike's commitment to appear in Wisconsin. Kohler had reluctantly declined a primary run against McCarthy, whom he disliked personally. The three envoys professed to be worried mainly about the Wisconsin ticket; Eisenhower, a proud man, was not pleased to be thus harried.

It is on the record that the general demanded to see McCarthy and that the two met alone for half an hour, face-to-face, in a suite at Peoria's Hotel Pere Marquette. But what happened in the meeting is disputed. Afterward McCarthy said only that there had been a "very, very pleasant conversation." Kevin McCann, an Eisenhower aide, recalled years later that he had been in a hallway outside and had listened while Eisenhower "just took McCarthy apart. I never heard the general so cold-bloodedly skin a man. The air turned blue—so blue in fact that I couldn't sit there listening. McCarthy said damned little. He just groaned and groaned."[28]*

No doubt mindful of the Jenner incident, Eisenhower refused to be photographed with McCarthy. The next day, as the train headed into Wisconsin, Kohler and the senator entered Eisenhower's private car, and Ike repeated to them his opposition to "un-American methods in combating communism." He also told McCarthy that in Wisconsin "I'm going to say that I disagree with you."

"If you say that, you'll be booed," McCarthy warned—almost incredible effrontery in speaking to the victor of World War II and a presidential nominee.

"I've been booed before and being booed doesn't bother me," Eisenhower replied.[29]

In Green Bay, however, he did not directly disagree with the senator or even mention him. He affirmed that his

---

* I knew McCann as a great admirer of Eisenhower—probably not so great that he would have invented this story. But since he told no reporters about it in 1952 and told no one until years after the fact, it seems possible that an aging memory might have embellished it a little.

administration would weed out any Reds in government but said it would insure that "American principles of trial by jury, of innocence until proof of guilt, are all observed." At Appleton Eisenhower did allow McCarthy to introduce him, but the senator wisely constrained himself to the bare-bones statement: "I wish to present to the people of my home city the next President of the United States, General Dwight Eisenhower."

Again, the presidential nominee did not mention McCarthy. The issue of his defense of Marshall, however, had not been settled. Later that day, with the Milwaukee address scheduled for the evening, Kohler and Senator William Knowland of California, a McCarthy admirer who was on the train, took it up with Sherman Adams, the former governor of New Hampshire and later White House chief of staff. They argued to Adams that the Marshall statement was "gratuitous" because, as Kohler put it, "Everybody knows how Eisenhower feels about Marshall. This line is just out of place in this speech." Speechwriter Gabriel Hauge strongly disagreed, but Adams went to Eisenhower and recommended deletion.

The general had to consider more than his relationship with Marshall. In 1952 no one, probably including Eisenhower, questioned Joe McCarthy's political power. He was, moreover, a favorite of many of the Republican conservatives, who had just suffered a highly emotional defeat with Robert Taft and were only dutifully supporting Eisenhower. And Wisconsin could not be considered entirely safe for the Republican ticket since four of the last five Democratic presidential nominees had carried the state.

After thinking all this over, Eisenhower demanded, "Are you telling me that paragraph is out of place?"

"Yes, sir," replied Sherman Adams, who was always to the point.

"Then take it out."

Some press reports suggest that Eisenhower added, "I handled that subject pretty thoroughly in Denver two weeks ago. There's no reason to repeat it tonight."[30]

The speech text had not been given to the press aboard the train. But Bill Lawrence, an experienced *New York Times* political reporter, knew about the Marshall "line," from Fred Seaton, the future secretary of the interior. McCarthy himself, however, told Lawrence that it had been deleted—"wait and see," he insisted.

When Press Secretary Jim Hagerty distributed the text, Lawrence saw at once that McCarthy had been right; and he and other reporters could hear the general's silence for themselves when Eisenhower delivered the speech to a crowd of eighty-five hundred that night in Milwaukee. Lawrence featured the deletion in his page 1 story for the *Times* on October 4, 1952, and Eisenhower's surrender to McCarthy, as it was generally interpreted, became a national sensation—the low point, in retrospect, of the Eisenhower "crusade."[31]

So great was the press focus on the undelivered Marshall defense that the rest of Eisenhower's Milwaukee speech went almost unnoticed; in fact, it was perilously close to McCarthy's standard Red-scare rhetoric. Two decades of tolerance for communism reaching high places in Washington, Ike said, had meant "contamination in some degree of virtually every department, every agency, every bureau, every section of our government. It meant a government by men whose very brains were confused by the opiate of this deceit," resulting in the fall of China and the "surrender of whole nations" in Eastern Europe. And at home tolerance of communism had allowed national policy to be set by "men who sneered and scoffed" at the threat, allowing "its most ugly triumph—treason itself."

No wonder that after this double victory for the junior senator from Wisconsin, in his home state's largest city, McCarthy eagerly shook General Eisenhower's hand, grinning broadly, acting not at all like a man who had been "skinned" the day before. McCarthy well may have been encouraged to think Eisenhower no more formidable than he had thought Truman. And no wonder that Arthur Hayes Sulzberger, publisher of the *New York Times* and an early and important Eisenhower backer, telegraphed Sherman Adams:

"Need I tell you that I am sick at heart?"[32]

BEFORE AND AFTER his muzzling of Eisenhower in Wisconsin, McCarthy was much in evidence during the campaign of 1952. The senator had undergone stomach surgery in August but nevertheless won his September 9 primary by a margin of more than two to one, carrying all but two of Wisconsin's seventy-two counties.

Thereafter, he traveled to at least ten states on behalf of like-minded Republican candidates—notably, in Arizona for the newcomer Barry Goldwater, where Ernest McFarland was to be the second Democratic Senate leader in two consecutive elections to lose with Joe McCarthy campaigning against him. McCarthy even campaigned by tape recorder in North Dakota. But his efforts could not defeat Democratic senator Joseph O'Mahoney in Wyoming, or prevent the election to the Senate of Democrat Mike Mansfield in Montana, or save the Senate seat of McCarthy's ally the Republican Harry P. Cain in Washington, where Henry M. "Scoop" Jackson was elected instead.

McCarthy also stumped in Michigan for Representative Charles Potter, who defeated Democratic senator Blair Moody; in Missouri, where Stuart Symington, a Democrat and (like Scoop Jackson) a future McCarthy enemy, nevertheless was elected to the Senate; in Indiana (for Jenner, who barely won); and in West Virginia, where the McCarthy boom had been launched in February 1950. He spoke three times in Connecticut, where William Benton lost his seat to William Purtell, due less to McCarthy's appearances than to an Eisenhower landslide in the state.

On October 27 in Chicago, using seventy-five thousand dollars of his own campaign funds and without the official support of Eisenhower or the Republican Party, McCarthy bought airtime on a national radio/TV network to "expose," he said, Adlai Stevenson. The exposure, as usual with Mc-Carthy, was dramatic—four times the senator pretended to misspeak about "Alger . . . I mean Adlai"—but lacked proof. Democratic researchers later identified what they said were "at least 18 false statements" in this diatribe, but there was little doubt the speech was highly effective. Part of it, Mc-Carthy's attack on Americans for Democratic Action, made page 1 of the *New York Times* the next day. (A later ADA reply was printed on page 26.)

Strangely, McCarthy did not appear in Massachusetts, where John F. Kennedy defeated Republican senator Henry Cabot Lodge. During the Tydings hearings, Lodge had defended McCarthy but McCarthy denied Lodge's appeals for election help. It is not established whether he did so because he did not want to offend the large Irish Catholic constituency in Massachusetts (assumed to be for Kennedy) or because Joseph P. Kennedy, the Democratic candidate's father and a contributor to McCarthy's Wisconsin campaign, asked or paid him to stay out of the state. Both may have been true.

In Nevada, campaigning for Republican George "Molly" Malone, McCarthy made a bitter enemy of a local editor, Hank Greenspun, by calling him an "ex-Communist" when he meant—or so he claimed—to say "ex-convict." Greenspun shouted from the audience that McCarthy was "the most vicious type of demagogue" and later charged that the senator was drunk. It perhaps was a case of ironic justice that McCarthy's misstatement, if that was what it was, made an enduring enemy of Greenspun, who thenceforth never missed a chance to attack the senator, sometimes producing national headlines.

In 1952 McCarthyism, as it was becoming widely known, was perhaps even more prominent than it had been in 1950. GOP candidates, using the slogan K1C2 (Korea, Communism, and Corruption), resorted freely to the senator's tactics. Nixon was an eager leader of the assault. Eisenhower himself—as in the Milwaukee speech—sometimes dabbled in quasi-Red-scare rhetoric, calling for repudiation of the Yalta agreements and blasting the Truman administration for supposedly having left Korea vulnerable to the communists.[33]

NOT LEAST BECAUSE of the Democrats' twenty-year reign, 1952 was a Republican year. Ike and Nixon won about 55 percent of the more than 60 million votes cast and carried five states—Texas, Virginia, Tennessee, Florida, and Oklahoma—of the formerly "Solid South," heralding the ultimate shift of the old Confederacy into the Republican Party. The Republicans did not fare quite as well overall but managed to retake control of Congress, 221 to 213 in the House and 48 to 47 in the Senate. (Republican Wayne Morse decided to become an independent.)

Joseph R. McCarthy was returned to the paper-thin Senate Republican majority and thus became chairman of the Senate Committee on Government Operations. His personal political power appeared—somewhat deceptively—to have been greatly enhanced, particularly by the defeat of McFarland and by the supposed McCarthy influence in Connecticut, where Purtell had captured Benton's seat. In politics, of course, appearances not only count but often are more important than reality. In fact, for example, Benton polled as many votes in 1952 as he had in 1950, when McCarthy was not opposing him, and ran forty-one thousand votes ahead of the Stevenson-Sparkman ticket in Connecticut. Still, indisputably, Benton had lost, and Joe McCarthy was generally believed, with a degree of plausibility, to have "got" another old Senate adversary.

Most Republican right-wing candidates, however, whether winners or losers and in whatever state—even those in which McCarthy had campaigned personally—failed to match the Eisenhower-Nixon winning percentages. Even in Wisconsin, and despite his huge primary victory, McCarthy could not equal Eisenhower's triumph in the general election and actually ran *last* among the state's twelve Republican congressional candidates. The senator was strongly opposed by organized labor and by influential newspapers, while most other Wisconsin Republicans had no or only token opposition. Though McCarthy bested his Democratic opponent, he received more than a hundred thousand votes *less* than his 1946 total.

Even so, as Joseph R. McCarthy seized control of the Government Operations Committee while Ernest McFarland and William Benton departed the Senate, few had reason to dispute William S. White's conclusion in the *New York Times* on January 18, 1953, that Wisconsin's junior senator was "in a position of extraordinary power" owing to "his well-documented political successes." It was not quite three years after his Wheeling speech.

McCarthy was to have in 1953 one of his most widely publicized years—not as a minority gadfly but as a majority inquisitor. He seemed not entirely to have realized, or recognized, however, that the White House had become Republican, too. He continued to act at times as if the executive branch were the enemy.

It CAN BE SEEN in retrospect that the election of President Eisenhower tolled the bell for Joe McCarthy. But as 1952 turned to 1953, that consequence was entirely unanticipated. In the Senate a strong group of right-wing conservatives was determined to take advantage, at last, of their majority status—men like Styles Bridges of New Hampshire, Everett Dirksen of Illinois, William Jenner of Indiana, Herman Welker of Idaho, Karl Mundt of South Dakota, the newly elected Barry Goldwater—and of course Joe McCarthy.

Right-wingers, however—famous, outspoken, and largely cooperative though they were—did not constitute a majority of the majority, even if without them there was no Republican majority at all in a Senate so closely divided. The Republican moderate faction was also anxious to expose communism in government—not so much for ideological reasons as to vindicate their party and to keep the Democrats on the defensive—but was critical of McCarthy's and the right wing's unrestrained tactics. This group was not entirely cohesive either, though its ranks had been augmented by the election of several Eisenhower men, such as Prescott Bush of Connecticut and Thomas Kuchel of California. Nor did the moderates have a majority of the majority.

Thus, the Republican cohort, while numerically in control of the chamber, was divided and immobilized. That the Old Guard's Taft, Eisenhower's powerful opponent, had become the new majority leader was emblematic of the Republican split. Even before the new president was sworn in, Taft denounced Ike's legislative program with table-pounding emphasis.

If the majority was divided, what about the Democrats— a minority of only one? The political reality was that any united Democratic move against Joe McCarthy, or to curb McCarthyism, carried the risk of making anticommunism a partisan issue—of driving the divided Republicans together in defense and, worse, of suggesting to the nation that Senate Democrats wanted an end to McCarthyism because McCarthyism principally threatened *them* and whatever they might be covering up from the New Deal and Fair Deal days.

Moreover, the Democratic minority was also divided. The twenty-two conservatives from what were then the eleven solidly Democratic states of the old Confederacy (along with several tacit allies from the West—Hayden of Arizona, for instance) were usually an unbreakable bloc. They balanced, if they did not outvote, more liberal colleagues with less seniority and less political security from more volatile states. The most respected Democrat in the Senate in 1953 probably was Richard B. Russell of Georgia—and perhaps the most significant Democratic result of the 1952 election was that the new minority leader, succeeding the defeated Ernest McFarland, was Russell's close colleague Lyndon Baines Johnson of Texas.

Johnson was a political strategist of a high order who was slowly beginning to transcend his Texas background and southern alliances. He quickly recognized the enormous popularity Dwight Eisenhower was taking with him into the White House and—grasping also the divided nature of the Republican Senate majority on which the president theoretically had to rely—set Senate Democrats in Ike's support. Only with Democratic votes, mobilized and led by Minority Leader Johnson, could Eisenhower defeat—by one vote— the so-called Bricker Amendment,* which at the outset of the

---

* Named after its primary sponsor, Old Guard senator John Bricker, Taft's colleague from Ohio. The Bricker Amendment to the Constitution would have limited the effect of treaties on U.S. internal law.

new administration threatened to curtail the president's powers. Similarly, Democratic votes made possible the confirmation of Eisenhower's chosen ambassador to the Soviet Union,
Charles "Chip" Bohlen—a renowned Sovietologist and friend
of Eisenhower who had been Franklin Roosevelt's translator
at Yalta. The right wing could not stomach that last item from
Bohlen's history.

Minority Leader Johnson was under heavy pressure from
Democratic liberals, in the Senate and outside it, to move just
as strongly against Joe McCarthy. Johnson resisted, counsel-
ing patience but arousing not a little resentment among his
own troops—who believed their party had a duty to silence
McCarthy and would have the votes to do so with the aid of
a few Republican moderates. Johnson, however, doubted the
Russell-led conservative southerners were ready for an open
fight with an anticommunist crusader; and he knew the dangers inherent in a Democratic assault on the broader issue of
McCarthyism.

"At this juncture," LBJ told William S. White, "I'm not
about to commit the Democratic party to a high school debate on the subject, 'Resolved, that Communism is good for
the United States,' with my party taking the affirmative."[34]

Moreover, Johnson's millionaire backers in Texas—men
he counted on to finance his political career, men who had
learned to count on *him* for political favors—were also supporters of Joe McCarthy and his campaign to "root out" com-

munists in government. Johnson faced reelection in Texas in 1954; and despite his low personal opinion of Tailgunner Joe, he had a certain respect for the political power of McCarthyism (having recently engaged in it himself to defeat Truman's reappointment of Leland Olds to the Federal Power Commission). Less cautious politicians than Lyndon Johnson believed in 1953 that tangling with Joe McCarthy was politically dangerous. LBJ was not inclined to do it until he believed the time was right or unless his hand was forced.

Joe McCarthy was not as willing to bide his time. He had always been headlong; and the unfolding of events in 1953 suggests in retrospect that his newfound eminence fatally affected his judgment: his committee chairmanship in the Senate majority, the staff and perquisites to which he was thus entitled, his proven popular support, his impending marriage to the beautiful and impressive Jean Kerr, and, above all, Washington's belief in his political power (a faith the one-time Wisconsin underdog undoubtedly shared).

6

IN JUNE 1953 McCarthy's sloppy habits and impulsive style caught up with him. Even such a sympathizer as FBI director J. Edgar Hoover thought it necessary to warn the famous Red hunter that in the future his investigations ought to entail "a great deal of preliminary spade work" to produce enough "substantive facts" on which to proceed. McCarthy was sufficiently impressed to remove Francis Flanagan as the chief of staff of his Permanent Subcommittee on Investigations. But incautiously failing to consult Hoover about a replacement, he then demonstrated precisely the inadequate research against which Hoover had warned him and hired J. B. Matthews. The new chief of staff had helped McCarthy as far back as the 1950 Tydings subcommittee hearings. But the director remembered Matthews as a leaker and headline hunter from Matthews's earlier service with the House Committee on Un-American Activities. At about the time Mc-

Carthy hired him, moreover, Matthews published in the *American Mercury* a resounding attack on the Protestant clergy as the "largest single group supporting the Communist apparatus in the United States today."

Hoover saw at once that this was disastrous overreaching. Not only were millions of Americans devoted Protestants who resented seeing their entire leadership—and, by implication, themselves—besmirched; not only was McCarthy identified as an Irish Catholic; but many of the leaders Matthews indicted—including Bishop G. Bromley Oxnam of the District of Columbia—were well connected politically, the Protestant clergy forming a lobby that even Joe McCarthy, had he been sufficiently alert, might have hesitated to attack.

As quickly as had Hoover, the Eisenhower White House saw the mistake and welcomed it as an opening through which to attack McCarthy. A strong telegram of protest from the National Conference of Christians and Jews was solicited; and Emmet Hughes prepared a harsh response in which Ike asserted that "irresponsible attacks that sweepingly condemn the whole of any group of citizens are alien to America." This denunciation just beat McCarthy to the punch, as he announced that J. B. Matthews had been fired.

Harry Byrd, Democrat of Virginia—one of the great powers of the Senate in 1953 and, as it happened, a friend of Bishop Oxnam—served as a catalyst for McCarthy's backtrack. Byrd denounced Matthews, clearly McCarthy's man, as "a cheap demagogue willing to blacken the character of his fellow Americans for his own notoriety and personal gain." Southern Democrats John Stennis of Mississippi and Burnet Maybank of South Carolina (an old foe) also attacked McCarthy for the Matthews hiring; and McCarthy's own subcommittee voted four to three[*] to support Matthews's dismissal.[35]

These speeches by Byrd, Stennis, and Maybank, as well as McClellan's "aye" in the subcommittee vote, raised the question of whether the southern conservatives had had enough of Joe McCarthy. A year earlier, in April 1952, McCarthy had almost casually attacked Darrell St. Claire, chief clerk of the Rules Committee. Aged Carl Hayden of Arizona—president pro tem of the Senate and then chairman of the Rules Committee, a traditional ally of the southerners—had taken personal offense at his aide's name being bruited about. For no obvious reason, Russell of Georgia had warned colleagues against those who undermined "the American system of fair play"—a considerable irony, coming from the leader of the Senate's southern racist bloc. Other senators had interpreted Russell's words as a signal that the southerners were ready to lower the boom on Wisconsin's junior senator.[36]

IF SO, THEY DID NOTHING about it until, as an overconfident chairman in 1953, McCarthy damaged himself with the

---

[*] Republican Charles Potter of Michigan joined Democrats Stuart Symington, Henry Jackson, and John McClellan of Arkansas.

Matthews incident. In an astonishing display of his peculiar bravado, no sooner had the subcommittee supported Matthews's dismissal than Chairman McCarthy demanded at a closed session on July 10, 1953, the right to hire and fire staff without subcommittee approval. He asked for an immediate vote. McCarthy controlled the majority and therefore was rewarded with the hire-and-fire authority he sought by a four-to-three party-line vote. In response, however, the three Democrats—Jackson, Symington, and McClellan—boycotted subcommittee hearings for the rest of 1953. That, William S. White wrote in the *New York Times,* was "about as grave a step as can be imagined" in the Senate, as it constituted not only a personal slap at McCarthy but a political move that deprived him of bipartisan cover.*

In the summer of 1953, following the hiring and firing of J. B. Matthews, McCarthy's decline in status was further signaled—to closely watching insiders—by J. Edgar Hoover. When Truman and the Democrats held power, Hoover had been willing to furnish FBI information to McCarthy,† McCarran, and other Red hunters in both parties; Hoover not only shared their anticommunism but also knew that much

---

* July 11, 1953.

† In 1971 I interviewed Roy Cohn, formerly chief counsel to the McCarthy subcommittee, in his Charles Addams–like town house on the Upper East Side of New York. Cohn readily acknowledged that Hoover had provided information to McCarthy. But when I quoted him in the published article, Cohn heatedly denied having said any such thing.

FBI information had been illegally obtained—by wiretaps, "black bag jobs," and other surreptitious enterprises—and therefore could not be used for legal indictments or in court proceedings. Members of Congress could and would use such information in hearings, investigations, and McCarthy-style denunciations, thus serving Hoover's purposes. The director insisted, of course, that the source of the information the FBI provided Congress be kept confidential and even devised official procedures to conceal such transactions. In return, the FBI sometimes received transcripts of closed congressional sessions and other useful bits of information.

When Eisenhower and the Republicans took power in 1953, they intended to continue exposing for political effect what they said—and in many cases believed—were Red influences in the former Truman administration and the Democratic Party. Therefore, the Eisenhower Justice Department authorized Hoover to continue honoring, on a case-by-case basis, congressional requests for FBI assistance in investigating matters of subversion. The bureau did provide such assistance in some instances in 1953—for example, during McCarthy's well-publicized probe into the radio broadcasting service Voice of America, the propaganda arm of the State Department.

By the time of the Matthews incident in the summer of 1953, Hoover had become wary of this arrangement. He feared that zealous anti-Red Republicans in Congress were about to come into conflict with the more moderate Eisenhower, as they had with Truman, and the Bohlen confirmation battle made it clear that foreign policy would be a point of conflict. The director—Washington's premier bureaucrat—did not want to be caught in the middle of such an intraparty war; the above-the-battle, nonpartisan pretensions he maintained for his cherished FBI would be damaged if the bureau were seen to take sides, particularly against the popular Eisenhower.

Having for once learned a lesson, McCarthy carefully consulted Hoover when replacing Matthews as the subcommittee chief of staff. He sent his trusted aide Jean Kerr* to ask the director's concurrence in the appointment of Francis Carr, currently an FBI employee. The cautious Hoover said he would neither agree to nor disapprove of Carr; but if Carr should be chosen, his appointment might appear to the public to provide "a pipeline" into the FBI. That would force the bureau to be more "circumspect" in dealing with—that is, providing information to—the McCarthy subcommittee.

Miss Kerr, as she still would be for a few more weeks, had been entrusted by McCarthy with sensitive assignments back to his 1950 effort to unseat Millard Tydings in Maryland (in

---

* On September 29, 1953, at St. Matthew's Cathedral in Washington, McCarthy and Miss Kerr, twenty-nine, were married, with Vice President Nixon, CIA director Allen Dulles, Sherman Adams, and many members of Congress, including Senator John F. Kennedy of Massachusetts, in the audience. The Pope cabled congratulations.

which she was instrumental). In this case, inexplicably, she did not inform the chairman of Hoover's veiled warning; or perhaps she failed to consider it as such. In any case, Francis Carr was duly hired as the subcommittee's chief of staff.

As a consequence, Louis Nichols, an assistant FBI director and Hoover's liaison with Congress, had to tell McCarthy later that the FBI "would have to lean over backwards [to follow procedure] because if at any time the Committee came up with something having an FBI angle, the charge would be made that Carr was a pipeline." Hoover also severed his "close liaison" with McCarthy. A memo from bureau executives to the director, written in October 1953, confirmed that "since [Carr was appointed staff director] . . . no information has been furnished to this [McCarthy] Committee."[37]

ALREADY McCARTHY HAD seriously alienated the White House and moderate Republicans—among other things—with his persistent opposition to Bohlen's confirmation. Eisenhower had had finally to intervene, but Bohlen was approved only with the help of the Democrats. So, too, was James Bryant Conant, Ike's nominee for high commissioner in West Germany—and McCarthy had to be dissuaded by Vice President Nixon from actively opposing Conant's nomination.

With a $200,000 budget assigned to the Permanent Investigations Subcommittee for 1953, Chairman McCarthy and his counsel, Roy Cohn, became active inquisitors. As the other six senators of the subcommittee were either boycotting or frequently busy on other matters, McCarthy often acted as a one-man subcommittee—judge, jury, and prosecutor rolled into one—with Cohn as a sleepy-eyed but deadly henchman. Among those summoned for interrogation by the subcommittee or the chairman were African American poet Langston Hughes, mystery writer Dashiell Hammett, *New York Times* columnist James Reston, composer Aaron Copland, and almost anyone whose presence would yield publicity—virtually the only result of any of the hearings.

Langston Hughes presented a long and eloquent discourse on the difficulties blacks faced in the United States of the 1950s—until he was abruptly cut off by Everett Dirksen, who said, "I think we have enough background."[38] When Dashiell Hammett was asked whether his short story "Night Shade" reflected the "Communist line," he replied: "On the word 'reflect' I would say no. It didn't reflect it. It was against racism."[39] Copland said he was not sure what a "communist sympathizer" was but had never thought of himself as such, and Hughes confessed to never having read "beyond the introduction of the Communist Manifesto."[40]

Cohn's major contribution to the subcommittee turned out to be a huge mistake: he brought on to the staff as a "consultant" his boyfriend G. David Schine, the high-living but unqualified son of a wealthy family. What consulting Schine might have done for the Investigations Subcommittee is not clear. Years later, in his book about racketeering in America, Robert F. Kennedy—briefly a subcommittee staff member in 1953—echoed J. Edgar Hoover's sentiments, observing that "Cohn and Schine claimed they knew at the outset [of any probe] what was wrong, and they were not going to let the facts interfere. Therefore no real spade work . . . was ever undertaken."[41] Schine was to prove not just superfluous or an embarrassment but a fatal liability in McCarthy's later conflicts with the U.S. Army.*

In 1953, however, a mostly untroubled subcommittee conducted 117 executive sessions. With other senators seldom present to check him, McCarthy bullied many of the hundreds of witnesses heard, then met an eager press to describe what had happened—who supposedly had said what, and who had refused to answer questions or say anything. Public hearings might or might not follow, depending mostly, it now appears, on what further publicity McCarthy and Cohn believed they could derive from the subject.

Through the first half of the year, most of these inquiries amounted to very little, although in one lengthy inquiry into the management of State Department personnel files, McCarthy did force a substantial revamping in the department's

---

* The Cohn-Schine relationship led to rumors that McCarthy, too, was homosexual. In a sort of poetic justice, no evidence ever confirmed this suggestion.

procedures. Not, however, until he opened an investigation of the Voice of America (VOA)—which broadcast news and commentary in forty-six languages to the world abroad—did McCarthy reap the kind of publicity on which he and his sub-committee thrived.

The most memorable aspect of this public investigation took place in April 1953, when Cohn and Schine teamed up to inspect VOA-operated public libraries in foreign embassies. Their stated objective was to uncover communist or Red-tainted literature being offered in these libraries to the foreign public at U.S. taxpayers' expense. But McCarthy's young lieu-tenants took only seventeen highly publicized days—nine of which were spent in West Germany—for this delicate task and earned much derision in foreign capitals for their holiday-ing, fraternity-buddy style. By the end of their mission, they had accomplished little except to win for themselves much publicity back in the States and the enduring epithet "junke-teering gumshoes."

This label was pinned on them by Theodore Kaghan, deputy chief of public relations for High Commissioner Co-nant in Bonn. Kaghan had proved himself a strong anticommu-nist during service in Austria from 1947 to 1951, but he was to pay a high price for his coinage and his courage. As their li-brary tour came to an end, Cohn and Schine were so badly re-ceived by the British press that they stayed only five hours in London before returning to Washington, where—coincidence or not?—the VOA promptly announced the dismissal of 830 employees as part of a $4.3 million "retrenchment."[42]

Theodore Kaghan, having been predictably subpoenaed to a closed subcommittee session, arrived in Washington not long after Cohn and Schine. When the subcommittee met, Cohn—now on home ground—aggressively quizzed Kaghan on his early leftist tendencies; unintimidated, Kaghan called them "a case of political chickenpox which you are trying to make into an incurable disease." Nevertheless, the journalist was forced to resign from government employ, though he landed on his feet as UN correspondent for the *New York Post*.

"When you cross swords with Senator McCarthy," he commented, "you cannot expect to remain in the State Department."[43]

Ultimately, the State Department sent lists of proscribed books, including works of Langston Hughes and Jean-Paul Sartre, to the overseas libraries. Former high commissioner John J. McCloy was outraged; in a show of American political diversity, he had deliberately stocked some of the newly banned books in the Bonn library while he was high commissioner. On June 14, 1953, McCloy journeyed to Dartmouth College to intervene with President Eisenhower, the commencement speaker. McCloy told Eisenhower that librarians in Germany had burned some of the forbidden books. The president was following a kid-gloves policy in handling McCarthy, but he urged his Dartmouth audience:

Don't join the book-burners. Don't think you are going to conceal faults by concealing evidence that they ever existed. Don't be afraid to go in your library and read every book as long as that document does not offend your sense of decency. That should be the only censorship.

Eisenhower's liberal supporters and McCarthy's critics cheered this forthright defense of free speech—until at a news conference three days later, the president partially withdrew his objection to book burning and conceded:

If the State Department is burning a book which is an open appeal to everybody in those foreign countries to be a Communist, then I would say that falls outside the limits I was speaking [of] and *they can do what they please to get rid of them* [italics added].

The president said he didn't want to "propagate communist beliefs" with government money in government libraries; furthermore, he had not been referring to McCarthy, Cohn, or Schine at Dartmouth because, as he explained, "I never talk personalities."[44]

NEVERTHELESS, by the summer of 1953, it was clear that J. Edgar Hoover had sensed the future: the Eisenhower

White House and Joe McCarthy were on a collision course. McCarthy, for instance, was not happy about being barred from investigating the CIA, then headed by Allen Dulles, a leading wartime OSS agent and the brother of Secretary of State John Foster Dulles.

On July 9 Roy Cohn had demanded—as usual without advance notice to anyone save the chairman—that the CIA analyst William Bundy should testify before the McCarthy subcommittee. Bundy was a gold-plated Ivy Leaguer (Groton and Yale); a son of Harvey Bundy, the World War II adviser to Secretary of the Army Henry L. Stimson; and a son-in-law of former secretary of state Dean Acheson. William was the elder brother of McGeorge Bundy, then a dean at Yale, later national security adviser in the Kennedy and Johnson administrations, and even later head of the Ford Foundation.

The Bundy family position mattered less to McCarthy and Cohn than the fact that Bill Bundy was on record as having contributed four hundred dollars to the Alger Hiss defense fund. Allen Dulles, however, viewed their summons to Bundy as the opening shot of a McCarthy inquiry into the CIA—which it was. Dulles promptly dispatched Bundy out of town and into virtual hiding, telling McCarthy: "Joe, you're not going to have Bundy as a witness."

Dulles took the position that if his agents were forced to testify, their sources of information would dry up—hardly an asset to the national security McCarthy was supposedly protecting. But McCarthy refused to concede that the CIA was immune to inquiry.* Vice President Nixon, his foot-in-the-other-camp status again of value to the president, had to broker a deal: no CIA men would be forced to testify before McCarthy, but Dulles would order an internal review of the Bundy matter.† Any way this deal was examined, it was not to Joe McCarthy's advantage.[45]

By then McCarthy and Cohn, the assiduous investigators, were on another track. They had met with Hoover to discuss the possibility of investigating J. Robert Oppenheimer. The "father of the atomic bomb" was the subject of familiar charges of prewar leftist activities and of new allegations of postwar disloyalty in urging Truman to discontinue development of the hydrogen bomb. Owing to FBI taps on Oppenheimer's telephone, Hoover had better information and tried to cool McCarthy's enthusiasm. Such a controversial investigation should not be "prematurely gone into solely for the purpose of headlines," Hoover said.

---

* "If they say . . . that calling an employee of the CIA will endanger their operations, I think we should lean over backwards to go along with them," McCarthy told the subcommittee. "But a man who has a record [of backing Hiss] must appear." Ted Morgan, *Reds* (New York: Random House, 2001), p. 452.

† In the late fifties, having been eased out of the CIA but not the government, Bill Bundy was chairman of the National Goals Commission. He became an assistant secretary of state under presidents Kennedy and Johnson and was deeply involved in management of the war in Vietnam.

That, of course, was precisely McCarthy's purpose. Nevertheless, confronted with Hoover's warning, he backed off.
Later in 1953 Hoover circulated within the administration a
thick file of charges and an FBI dossier, both raising the question of Oppenheimer's loyalty. Pursued by Lewis Strauss, the
director of the Atomic Energy Commission (AEC), and by
Eisenhower, these charges resulted in the famous Oppenheimer hearings of 1954 and the suspension of the physicist's
"Q" clearance for classified matter—a suspension upheld by
Strauss's AEC, four to one. Major motives for this inquiry into
the loyalty of the nation's most distinguished scientist were
Strauss's personal animosity toward Oppenheimer and Eisenhower's fear that if he did not push the hearings, McCarthy
would conduct his own.

The president told James Hagerty, his press secretary,
"We've got to handle this so that all of our scientists are not
made out to be Reds. That goddamn McCarthy is just likely
to try such a thing."[46]

Thus, while McCarthy never officially went after the scientist who had led the Manhattan Project to build the
A-bomb during World War II, the name of J. Robert Oppenheimer may be fairly added to the list of those ruined by
Tailgunner Joe. Had McCarthy, his subcommittee, and Mc-
Carthyism not been prominent and powerful in Washington
in the 1950s, Oppenheimer might have been protected by the
president, who, instead, protected himself. Senator Clinton

Anderson, Democrat of New Mexico and a member of the AEC at the time, said its members—including Strauss—had bowed to "the McCarthy hysteria."[47]

As it was, the CIA and Oppenheimer cases added to the White House's growing fear and resentment of McCarthy, his tactics, and his potential to damage the administration. As for McCarthy, he must have wondered, as the Oppenheimer hearings progressed to their shabby ending, how he had been aced out of such a rich harvest of headlines. His affection for the Eisenhower administration and his admiration for J. Edgar Hoover could scarcely have been enhanced.

WHAT KEPT MCCARTHY out of direct participation in the Oppenheimer case was in large part his self-destructive entanglement with the U.S. Army—brought about mostly by Roy Cohn's infatuation with G. David Schine, the "consultant" Cohn had added to the subcommittee staff.

As early as July 1953, Chairman McCarthy—presumably pushed by Cohn—asked General Miles Reber, the army's liaison with Congress, to obtain a commission for Schine, who had no visible qualifications save a decent education and his relationship with Cohn. On July 15 a confident Schine personally renewed this application to Reber but found himself sent to the Pentagon dispensary, instead, for a physical exam. On July 23, despite his connections, Schine was informed that he had been found "not qualified."

Later that summer a memo of a conversation between Sam Papich, an FBI liaison, and Assistant Secretary of State Walter Bedell Smith, Eisenhower's World War II chief of staff, was filed within the bureau. The memo stated that Roy Cohn had told Smith on several occasions that he and McCarthy wanted Schine to have an army commission *without* having to take basic training. (Back in 1942 even Judge Joe McCarthy had not sought such privilege.) When Smith refused, Cohn asked if Schine might be appointed to the CIA; Smith demurred again and no doubt considered an unseemly matter to be closed.

Before McCarthy's marriage on September 29, 1953, he and Cohn had initiated a series of hearings focused on the army, particularly on supposed subversive activities at Fort Monmouth, New Jersey (and not necessarily connected to the Schine matter). The subcommittee Democrats' boycott was continuing, Republican members often were busy with other affairs, and most of these hearings were a one-man show for McCarthy. Little information about subversion was obtained, and none about espionage. Though some civilian employees lost their jobs as alleged "security risks," most were later reinstated by the courts or by the army.

The hearings nevertheless worried Secretary of the Army Robert Stevens, an old Eisenhower supporter and a former businessman innocent of any experience in or taste for bureaucratic infighting. Stevens decided on two courses of action:

appeasement of McCarthy when possible and the appointment of a South Dakota lawyer, John Adams (no relation to Sherman Adams), as a special liaison to deal with the subcommittee and its chairman.

The McCarthy-Cohn efforts on behalf of David Schine eventually began to focus on Secretary Stevens, an obvious soft touch. Stevens or someone else delayed induction for Schine, who finally was forced on November 3, 1953, to enter the army as a private, at Fort Dix. Even after that, innumerable special privileges were sought and allowed for the new inductee, including more weekend passes than privates usually could obtain, a car and a driver to take him to New York on these occasions, relief from KP duty and guard detail, and frequent absences—sometimes for most of the night—from the post. If Secretary Stevens did not personally order these privileges, it was well known among the troops at Fort Dix that Private Schine was an influential character—his perks being obvious and his unwise boasts about them having been widely circulated.

Schine's privileges were not accidental, though it's hard to assign specific responsibility for specific preferences. When John Adams inquired of Roy Cohn what would happen if Schine were sent overseas, the arrogant Cohn, by then a power at McCarthy's side, replied bluntly: "Stevens is through as Secretary of the Army. . . . [W]e'll wreck the Army . . . if you pull a dirty, lousy, stinking, filthy, shitty double cross like that."[48]

In January 1954 Secretary Stevens left for a month's tour in the Far East. At about that time, Cohn learned from Adams that Schine was to be sent to Camp Gordon, Georgia (perhaps, to a confirmed New Yorker like Roy Cohn, farther away than "overseas"), for five months at Provost Marshal school. The next day Francis Carr called Adams and told him that Cohn was angry about Schine's assignment and that Cohn wanted to question six army loyalty board members and was willing to subpoena them.

Not unnaturally, Adams concluded that these matters were linked: Cohn wanted to quiz the army board members *because* the army was sending his boyfriend to Georgia—tit for tat. Adams immediately sought advice from Attorney General Brownell. At a follow-up conference in Brownell's office in January 1954, less than a year after Eisenhower's inauguration, Adams found, in addition to the attorney general, three of the administration's principal political figures: Chief of Staff Sherman Adams, UN ambassador (and former senator) Henry Cabot Lodge,* and Gerald Morgan of the White House–congressional liaison staff. Vice President Nixon, a political troubleshooter of equivalent stature, apparently was not wanted at what turned into a strategy session on the subject of McCarthy versus the U.S. Army.[†]

---

* For whom McCarthy had *not* campaigned in 1952.

[†] "It's [Eisenhower's] army," Jim Hagerty confided to his diary, "and he doesn't like McCarthy's tactics at all." Robert H. Ferrell, ed., *The Diary of James C. Hagerty* (Bloomington: Indiana University Press, 1983), p. 20.

John Adams gave the group an account of the pressures the chairman and Roy Cohn had brought on behalf of David Schine. The White House emissaries ordered him to draft a chronology of what they recognized as serious blunders that could be used in Eisenhower's developing anti-McCarthy campaign.

That same month McCarthy stumbled on a case that heightened his conflict with the army. A service dentist named Irving Peress had been promoted to major at Camp Kilmer, New Jersey, although he had been a communist (actually, a Trotskyite) in private life. He had lied to the army about his affiliation, then claimed Fifth Amendment protection. McCarthy's interest in Peress—which caused the dentist again to "take the Fifth"—resulted in Peress's honorable discharge but did not put an end to McCarthy's inquiry.

McCarthy's repeated, almost comical demands to know "who promoted Peress?" quickly made the affair a headline case. In New York in February 1954, McCarthy pursued the matter in another of his one-man hearings, this time confronting General Ralph Zwicker, Camp Kilmer's commanding officer.

Wearing his beribboned army uniform, Zwicker tried to clarify one question by asking: "Do you mean how do I feel about communists?"

Apparently in a worse-than-usual mood, McCarthy snapped back: "I mean exactly what I asked you, General. . . . Anyone with the brains of a five-year-old child can understand the question."

He then demanded to know whether Zwicker believed a general should be relieved of duty because he had authorized an honorable discharge for someone he knew to be a communist. When Zwicker said no, McCarthy exploded:

"Then, General, you should be relieved from any command. Any man who has been given the honor of being promoted to general and who says[,] 'I will protect another general who protected communists,' is not fit to wear that uniform, General."*

Zwicker had been fit to wear his uniform on D-day in 1944 as one of Eisenhower's officers going ashore in France for the invasion of Europe. McCarthy's tirade resulted in national headlines and more presidential animosity—as well as a rare fit of resistance from Secretary Stevens, who ordered Zwicker not to testify further. This departure from Stevens's customary appeasement apparently whetted McCarthy's appetite for combat: in retaliation, he ordered Stevens to take the stand, intending to steer the issue from Zwicker back to Peress.

Alarmed but still accommodating, Stevens—like a lamb to the slaughter—went willingly to a "compromise" meeting held on February 24 in Everett Dirksen's Senate office. McCarthy, Dirksen, Mundt, and Potter confronted the secretary.

---

* McCarthy's sympathetic biographer Arthur Herman has pointed out that the senator and his new wife had been in a taxi accident the day before, that McCarthy had spent the previous night with her in the hospital, and that McCarthy had had no lunch. But Herman also speculates that McCarthy had been drinking.

The compromise between such an innocent and three right-wing sharks (Potter was not in the same ferocious class as his colleagues) was almost foregone: Stevens not only agreed in writing to let Zwicker testify again but also to disclose the names of everyone involved in Peress's promotion and discharge. Newspapers eagerly branded the "compromise" an administration "surrender" to McCarthy.

The chairman told a reporter that Stevens could not have given in "more abjectly if he had gotten down on his knees." When McCarthy received a call from Bill Lawrence, who had been assigned to what he called the "sewer beat" for the *New York Times,* the senator inquired genially:

"Bill, have you ever thought you'd like to be a general?"

"Good God, no, Joe. Why?"

"Well . . . I can fix it. I'm running the Army now."[49]

Eisenhower obviously did not agree. He helped draft a strong statement in which Stevens denied surrendering and promised to defend army personnel. The secretary read this statement at the White House, and Hagerty told reporters the president stood fully behind it. Eisenhower showed support for Stevens in various other ways, but McCarthy characteristically refused to back down. On March 4, 1954, at a televised meeting of his subcommittee, he declared in an obvious reference to Zwicker that "if a stupid, arrogant or witless man in a position of power appears before our committee and is found to be aiding the Communist party, he will be exposed."

Eisenhower was not the general or the president to accept

this defiance; on March 2 he had instructed the Justice Department to prepare a legal brief on the president's power to
order subordinates not to testify. This "executive privilege"
study, coming after the January meeting in which John Adams
and administration political strategists had decided to capital-
ize on the army's special treatment of David Schine, represented a second and profoundly important step in the
now-determined White House war on Joe McCarthy.[50]

ON JANUARY 25, 1954, the boycotting Democrats—McClellan, Symington, and Jackson—had returned to the Permanent
Investigations Subcommittee after demanding conditions that,
when closely examined, were a setback for the chairman.
Henceforth, it had been agreed, hiring and firing would be
done by a majority, not by McCarthy alone; the Democrats,
moreover, would have their own counsel—ultimately Robert
Kennedy—and no public hearings would be held without
unanimous minority consent. In return for these concessions,
McCarthy received nothing more than Democratic Party support for the subcommittee's annual budget, against which
only William Fulbright of Arkansas ("Half-bright," McCarthy
liked to call him) proved willing to vote. Would the Johnson-
led Democrats, in any circumstances, have denied funding to
a subcommittee investigating communist subversion—subversion supposedly by Democrats, at that? Despite initial opposition to the subcommittee budget by Chairman Hayden of
the Rules Committee, it seems unlikely.

Through the winter of 1953 and 1954, John Adams's chronology of McCarthy's and Cohn's efforts to obtain preferential treatment for David Schine lay in a drawer of Adams's Pentagon desk, a time bomb waiting to explode. On March 9 the White House enlisted Republican Charles Potter—a paraplegic veteran who, it turned out, had deplored McCarthy's attack on Zwicker—to ask Secretary of Defense Charles Wilson to release the Schine report.

This day, too, Senator Ralph Flanders of Vermont—a McCarthy critic since the sugar debate of 1947—attacked McCarthy on the Senate floor (which in 1951 or 1952 would have been unthinkable even for Flanders, who was soon to retire). The Wisconsin senator "dons his war paint," Flanders declared sarcastically. "He goes into his war dance. He emits his war whoops. He goes forth to battle and proudly returns with the scalp of a pink Army dentist."

America, Eisenhower wrote Flanders, "needs to hear more voices like yours."[51] That night it did, as Edward R. Murrow broadcast on the CBS network a devastating *See It Now* report damning McCarthy's smears and lies with text and film. The opposition to McCarthyism that had existed since Wheeling had expanded;* the public response—*against* McCarthy— was overwhelming. A half century later, probably no television

---

* McCarthy's Gallup Poll approval rating already had fallen to 46 percent. The Murrow broadcast was the first of four devoted to McCarthyism, to only one of which the senator was given airtime to respond.

program has had a greater impact on a more receptive public. Then, on March 11, like the second half of a one-two punch, the Schine chronology was released by the Pentagon. The report specified fifty-four counts of improper pressure on the army from McCarthy and, especially, from Roy Cohn.

Any other fighter might have gone down for the count. Joe McCarthy was on his feet quickly, counterpunching. Almost overnight he and his staff produced a series of staff memos supposedly proving that *the army* had been pressuring *McCarthy*—not the other way around. In effect, the memos seemed to show that the army was holding Schine as a "hostage" to force McCarthy to drop his inquiries into subversion at Fort Monmouth and elsewhere.*

Faithful Karl Mundt quickly proposed an impartial Senate inquiry into which account was to be believed—Adams's chronology or McCarthy's memos. However, in a March 16 executive session,† with its full Democratic membership present, the Investigations Subcommittee voted to conduct its own inquiry into these disputed events—and specified that Chairman Joseph R. McCarthy could not preside over an investigation of himself; he would have to step down. He did,

---

* Testimony by Roy Cohn during the Army-McCarthy hearings strongly suggested that the memos were fictitious. An oral history interview of Willard Edwards tends to confirm the memos' inauthenticity (State Historical Society of Wisconsin, January 17, 1976).

† Potter apparently sided with the Democrats in this meeting.

announcing that Mundt would wield the gavel. In this case, the tail would wag the dog; but there was another, perhaps more important question: Could Joe McCarthy vote on his own fate?

Eisenhower told a news conference, "If a man is party to a dispute, he does not sit in judgment on his own case." With this pronouncement ringing in his ears, McCarthy unexpectedly agreed to step aside again, with another close friend and disciple, Henry Dworshak of Idaho, moving temporarily on to the subcommittee to take McCarthy's seat and vote. But McCarthy would remain at the committee table, reserving his right to cross-examine and even subpoena witnesses.

More important than any of this maneuvering was the advice given to John McClellan, the subcommittee's senior Democrat, by Minority Leader Lyndon Johnson. Perhaps having absorbed the public effect of Ed Murrow's *See It Now* broadcast, LBJ counseled McClellan that no matter what other concessions the subcommittee Democrats might have to make, they should insure that the Army-McCarthy hearings were broadcast *in full* on national television.

"Two minutes a night . . . wasn't enough," Johnson believed. "McCarthy had to be seen day after day during the entire hearings on the Army."[52]

7

★ ★ ★

LBJ WAS RIGHT. The press had done more than any American institution to elevate Joe McCarthy into a formidable national figure; but Johnson sensed that television, just emerging in the 1950s as the power arm of "the media," could destroy the junior senator from Wisconsin.

The nation's air waves, however, were not to be so nearly saturated with the Army-McCarthy hearings as Johnson had hoped and as is sometimes recalled in political and broadcast lore. The two dominant networks, CBS and NBC, found that dropping their extensive and lucrative daytime programming to provide gavel-to-gavel coverage of a mere Senate hearing would be prohibitively expensive. Though NBC did carry the first day's sessions live and in full, these networks thereafter provided only the nighttime summaries that LBJ considered insufficient.

The full hearings schedule—188 hours—was broadcast

as a public service only by the ABC and DuMont* television networks, which meant that not all areas received complete daily coverage. Cable costs prevented ABC from sending its feed—provided by WMAL of Washington—farther west than Omaha, Nebraska. Thus viewers in Los Angeles, for instance, could see only still photos in the broadcast of ABC's affiliate, KTLA, although the station did carry the live sound track from Washington.

Even so, as the only Army-McCarthy show in town, KTLA's truncated coverage got smash-hit ratings. In fact, the live Army-McCarthy coverage, even with its inevitable dull spots, became as riveting to many of those who could see it as, in later years, some viewers found the O.J. Simpson murder trial. Ratings climbed as the hearings continued over thirty-six days; ultimately, a Trendex survey found that the broadcasts were attracting a 68 percent share of the television audience. In New York City, daytime viewing rose 50 percent above normal; in St. Louis, when a Cardinals-Dodgers baseball game preempted the hearings, nearly a thousand callers protested; in Houston, after NBC decided against continuing live coverage, its local station made a maverick deal with ABC for the daily feed. (Owing to high costs, however, this unusual arrangement was soon canceled.)

ABC's decision to broadcast the hearings in full cost the

---

* The weak DuMont network was to go out of existence in 1955.

network an estimated $500,000 (in 1950s dollars). But Robert Kintner, ABC's chieftain, undoubtedly considered the money well spent, given the notoriety, prestige, and public encomia the broadcasts earned. This kind of gain was particularly important in 1954 for what was then an also-ran network seeking rough parity with the majors.

The power of television, even as limited by financial considerations at NBC and CBS, was so graphically demonstrated by the public reception for the Army-McCarthy broadcasts that Congress rather typically took alarm. Tom Hennings of Missouri, a senator in 1954 and one of Joe McCarthy's severest critics, grumped that Senate business should not be allowed "to compete with *John's Other Wife* or . . . *Dragnet.*"

As a result of such elitist views, and of the soon-demonstrated public reaction against one of its members, Congress did not allow broadcasts of the hearings later in 1954 in which a special bipartisan committee chaired by Arthur Watkins, Republican of Utah, considered McCarthy's censure. And despite scattered broadcasts of the so-called Rackets Committee hearings between 1957 and 1959,[53] it was not until *twenty years* later—in 1973 and 1974, during the Watergate scandal and impeachment proceedings against President Nixon—that Congress again allowed extensive live television coverage of its workings.

———

THE ARMY-MCCARTHY HEARINGS began on April 22, 1954, in the ornate Senate Caucus Room. Necessary preliminaries included Mundt taking the chair, Dworshak assuming McCarthy's vote, and the appointments of counsel: Ray Jenkins, a growling, crew-cut Tennessee criminal lawyer, for the Republican majority; Robert Kennedy, a former McCarthy aide, for the Democratic minority; and Joseph N. Welch, a little-known Boston lawyer, for the U.S. Army. Roy Cohn had suggested that if he or McCarthy were interrogated by either side, each should act as his own counsel. Good lawyers would have advised against Cohn's proposal; McCarthy, who was not a good lawyer, accepted it.

Cameras were in place, the committee members were strategically arranged for TV exposure, WMAL's sound truck was parked outside, and about a hundred spectators* had been allowed to sit among the hundreds of Congress members, army officers, and officials who were to make up the permanent in-the-room audience. Bryson Rash of WMAL provided necessary commentary, and Gunnar Back of ABC was ready to interview interesting persons and offer background to fill unavoidable breaks in the action. The celebrated Walter Winchell sat with the press, wearing his trademark fedora. Across the country an immense jury of the public was available to pass judgment, not only on the claims of

---

* Long lines of citizens waited every day for a seat to become available.

McCarthy versus the U.S. Army, but ultimately and essen-
tially—though this was unforeseen—on McCarthyism itself.

General Reber was the first witness. But even before he
could be called, Joe McCarthy demonstrated how he intended to proceed: "Point of Order! Mr. Chairman!" he called
out in his familiar nasal voice, going on to declare that since
Secretary Stevens and John Adams were civilians, their
charges against him should not be labeled as coming from the
Department of the Army. A few minutes later, McCarthy interrupted Reber's testimony to attack the general's brother
Sam as a possible "bad security risk."

The hearings continued for more than a month, during
which McCarthy's frequent "point of order" interruptions,
often followed by irrelevant or unsupported observations, became an irritating pattern. Despite his many TV appearances,
the senator seemed not to realize, in those early days of the
medium, that from beyond the Caucus Room a huge home
audience was watching and judging—not just the facts but
him. In later years a documentary about the hearings was entitled, not inappropriately, *Point of Order.*

Secretary Stevens followed Reber to the stand and in
four days of testimony described in excruciating detail a
"persistent, tireless effort to obtain special consideration and
privileges" for Private G. David Schine.[54] But four days were
not enough for McCarthy; using his privilege of cross-

examination, he kept Stevens under brusque interrogation for nine more days. Even then he was unable to shake the mild-mannered secretary from his basic, damning testimony.

Apart from such hostile witnesses, the continuing sessions—conducted in a haze of tobacco smoke—were not kind to McCarthy. He snarled at committee members, insulted Stevens, griped at Mundt, tried to "strike from the record" remarks that had been heard by the TV audience, and earned from *New York Times* journalist James Reston the judgment that "the senator from Wisconsin is a bad-tempered man" who was being hurt by both his "manner and his manners." No politician today would so conduct himself before the unforgiving cameras and the millions watching in their living rooms.

McCarthy was his own worst enemy, his unappealing behavior exacerbated to some extent by great stress. His sympathetic biographer has observed that during most of the hearings, he suffered

> . . . from constant stomach complaints and sinus headaches. . . . Then there was the drinking. . . . What had been a shot of bourbon at work was now a tumbler. Where he had once relied on a surreptitious drink to get through a public speech, he now needed several to get through a morning of normal work. . . . When the hearings adjourned at 4:30 P.M. he would

gather with his aides for several hours, then eat a hurried dinner before returning to the office to look at
more files and plan strategy for the next day. . . . Mc-
Carthy would often sit up all night, shifting papers
and sipping straight vodka until 6:00 A.M.[55]

When Ray Jenkins introduced a photograph showing
Stevens and Schine smiling at each other—an attempt to por-
tray the secretary of the army and the private as friends—a
strong whiff of the old McCarthy campaign against Millard
Tydings in Maryland permeated the hearing. The photo had
been cropped—doctored?—as Joseph Welch was able to
demonstrate. He showed the Caucus Room and the home audience an enlarged print of the original picture, in which
Stevens was smiling at a *third person*—a Colonel Bradley.
Bradley had been cut out of the photo Jenkins had introduced
on McCarthy's behalf "as if it were honest," Welch said.*

  The bow-tied Boston lawyer was proving to be something
like McCarthy's equal in dexterity and innuendo. When a Mc-
Carthy aide, for instance, questioned where the uncropped
photo had been found, Welch replied: "Did you think it came
from a pixie?"

---

* The photo may have been cropped by army photographers for benign reasons, as McCarthy's aides argued. Even if so, it did not support the idea that
Stevens and Schine had been friends. Reporters and others not unreason-
ably recalled the photo McCarthy and/or his staff had "doctored" during the
1950 Tydings campaign.

McCarthy broke in: "Will counsel for my benefit define—
I think he might be an expert on that—what a pixie is?"

Welch could hardly have foreseen such an opening, but,
without pause, he riposted: "I would say, senator, that a pixie
is a close relative of a fairy."

A reaction shot aired by the ABC engineer Ed Scherer
caught McCarthy grinning gamely—but Roy Cohn, sitting
beside the senator, looking as though he had been slapped.[56]
Cohn realized, if his boss didn't, that Welch had implicitly
raised the homosexuality issue and the relationship widely
suspected between Cohn and Schine—and maybe even between McCarthy and either or both of the aides.[*]

The bad impression made by the Stevens-Schine-Bradley
photo—whether routinely cropped or doctored—was rein-
forced at the May 4 session when McCarthy produced two
and a quarter pages he cited as a copy of a letter from J. Edgar
Hoover to the head of U.S. Army Intelligence. The letter
named thirty-five Fort Monmouth employees suspected of
subversion. Welch, surprised, ordered a search of army files
and found that Hoover had indeed sent such a letter—but
that the original was *fifteen pages* long.

McCarthy's version was only a summary, and Welch

---

[*] McCarthy always stood by Cohn, giving rise to unsupported rumors of a
sexual relationship. In *Rave* magazine, June 1954, Hank Greenspun, pursuing his vendetta, wrote that McCarthy, "judged by the very standards by
which he judges others, is a security risk on the grounds of homosexual
associations."

called it "a carbon copy of precisely nothing . . . a perfect phony." Since the substance of the letter had not been altered in the summary, Welch's description was an overstatement reminiscent of McCarthy's own tactics. Yet the short summary had been presented as a copy of an original, and the exposure seemed to many to show McCarthy using false documents as well as faked photographs.*

THE HEAVIEST BLOW was to hit McCarthy after John Adams of the Department of the Army took the stand. Adams was sworn in on May 13, about three weeks into the hearings, and fully backed Stevens's testimony as to the unprecedented pressures exerted on behalf of Private Schine. Then, on Friday, May 14, Adams mentioned almost in passing the January 21 meeting of administration political strategists in Herbert Brownell's office. Symington of Missouri wondered why Lodge, the UN ambassador, had been involved in a domestic matter. But before Adams could answer, if he had intended to, Welch broke in to say that Adams had been instructed not to disclose details of what had been a high-level discussion within the executive department.

---

* Viewer antipathy to McCarthy may have had unfortunate ethnic roots. Thomas Doherty believes viewers saw the establishmentarian Welch as "the anti-McCarthy, the anti-Cohn, the genteel WASP against the loutish Mick and the pushy Jew." *Cold War, Cool Medium* (New York: Columbia University Press, 2003), p. 192.

On that unsatisfactory note—instructed by whom?—the subcommittee adjourned for the weekend, informing Adams that he should return on Monday, May 17, with his instructions in writing. What he brought to the Monday hearing may have seemed to TV viewers and to some in the Caucus Room as no more than legalese; but lawyers on the subcommittee knew at once that President Dwight D. Eisenhower had landed a body blow to Joe McCarthy.

What Adams gave the subcommittee was a copy of a letter from Eisenhower to Secretary of Defense Charles E. Wilson. In it the president stated that executive departments were to furnish Congress full information about their policies but *not* "conversations, communications and documents" about how and why those policies had been decided upon. "It is essential to efficient and effective administration," Eisenhower asserted rather grandly, "that employees of the Executive Branch be in a position to be completely candid with each other on official matters." If they feared their deliberations might be made public, they might not be so candid—in which case, the president wrote, he would not receive their best advice. The letter was a sweeping statement of what became popularly known as "executive privilege," and it meant—if Eisenhower could make it stick—that "investigators" such as Joe McCarthy would no longer have unlimited ability to inquire into internal administration affairs.

In a meeting at the White House on the same day that
the subcommittee pondered the Eisenhower-to-Wilson letter,
the president told Republican congressional leaders the facts
of life as he claimed to see them: "Anyone who testifies as to
the advice he gave me won't be working for me that night,"
he asserted. "I will not allow people around me to be subpoenaed and you might as well know it now."

Knowland, the Senate Republican leader and a McCarthy
supporter, momentarily defended, probably rightly so, Congress's subpoena power. But Eisenhower replied bluntly: "My
people are not going to be subpoenaed."[57]

Eisenhower *did* make his new doctrine stick, more through
personal prestige and political eminence than legal certainty.
Historical research has found few, if any, precedents for his
version of executive privilege, and stronger congressional,
press, and academic protests than Knowland's soon were
heard. But McCarthy's perceived excesses lent the order an
air of necessity and legitimacy—at least to McCarthy's critics—that it might not have had in other circumstances or if
issued by a different president. In 1954, moreover, Dwight
Eisenhower was virtually unchallengeable. Even someone as
reputable as John McClellan of Arkansas, no doubt speaking
for many southern conservatives, was all but ignored when he
called Eisenhower's declaration "one of the gravest mistakes
this administration has made."

The Eisenhower order has largely withstood academic

and legislative arguments, limited exceptions approved by
federal courts,* and presidents' decisions not always to follow
it. "A claim born of desperation in 1954," constitutional histo-
rian Raoul Berger wrote in 1974, "had ripened by 1956 into a
time-honored principle."[58] Though less honored today, the
order is still widely regarded as a "principle," if one neither
carved in stone nor derived from the Constitution, as Berger
has argued persuasively.

In 1954 even McCarthy—outgunned for once—seemed
to submit: "I must admit I am somewhat at a loss to know
what to do at this moment."[59] He was not long at a loss, however; Joe McCarthy seldom was. On May 27, ten days after
Adams disclosed the executive-privilege letter, McCarthy
again breathed fire and defiance. He called on "the two million federal workers . . . to give us any information which they
have about graft, corruption, Communists, treason. . . . There
is no loyalty to a superior officer which can tower above and
beyond their loyalty to the country."

McCarthy, of course, had his own definition of "loyalty
to the country," one that caused Eisenhower to lose his
barracks-room temper. As he stomped about the Oval Office,
the president declared to Hagerty that

---

* President Nixon frequently invoked the Eisenhower order; but in 1974
Nixon could not shelter, under that doctrine, secret tape recordings of his
meetings and telephone conversations that were the subject of a criminal
(the Watergate) inquiry by court-appointed prosecutors.

. . . this amounts to nothing but a wholesale subversion of public service. . . . McCarthy is making exactly the same plea of loyalty that Hitler made to the
German people. Both tried to set up personal loyalty
within the Government while both were using the
pretense of fighting Communism. . . . I think this is
the most disloyal act we have ever had by anyone in
the government of the United States.

Brownell issued a strong statement, backed by the White
House:

The executive branch has sole and fundamental responsibility to enforce the law and presidential orders
[and it] cannot be usurped by any individual who may
seek to set himself above the laws of our land, or override orders of the President . . . to federal employees.*

As if to put an exclamation point to these responses, Edward R. Murrow broadcast another *See It Now* on the CBS
network, inveighing against what he portentously called "an
elaborate system of informers" providing a senator with
"stolen information." A few weeks later, at Columbia Univer-

---

* Even in the context of the McCarthy era and its challenges to constitutional
principles, it may be questioned whether to "override" the orders of the president is the same as setting oneself above the laws of the land.

sity's commencement exercises, Eisenhower denounced "those who seek to establish over us thought control"—whether foreign states or "demagogues thirsty for personal power and public notice." True to form, however, the president did not name Joseph R. McCarthy or engage in personalities.

THE ARMY-MCCARTHY HEARINGS, of course, were far from over, and the most public denigration of McCarthy was yet to come, courtesy of Joseph N. Welch.

The staff of Hale and Dorr, Welch's Boston law firm, included a lawyer named Fred Fisher. In his college years, Fisher had been a member of the National Lawyers Guild (NLG), a supposed communist front. Welch deliberately had not involved Fisher in the hearings, but this aspect of Fisher's past had been disclosed in a *New York Times* article. Early in June, however, Roy Cohn and Welch made a deal: if Cohn would not bring up Fisher and his NLG past, Welch would not make an issue of the fact that Cohn had twice avoided the draft. Cohn later wrote that Senator McCarthy had agreed to the pact.[60]

On June 9 the agreement suddenly fell apart. Welch was questioning Cohn in a jocular tone about Cohn's eagerness to expose communists and asked:

"If I told you now we had a bad situation at [Fort] Monmouth, you would want to cure it by sundown, if you could, wouldn't you?"

Sounding equally jocular, Cohn said he was sure he could *not* cure it.

Welch put in another dig: "Whenever you learn of [communists or subversives] from now on, Mister Cohn, I beg of you, will you tell somebody about them quick?"

At that Joe McCarthy erupted—not this time with a point of order but with an angry reply to Welch's mockery:

". . . in view of Mister Welch's request . . . I think we should tell him that he has in his law firm a young man named Fisher . . ."

Cohn tried to interrupt, but McCarthy drove ahead:*
". . . whom he recommended, incidentally, to do work for this committee . . ."

Mundt tried to say that Welch had not so recommended Fisher, but McCarthy refused to be quieted:

". . . who has been for a number of years a member of the organization which was named, oh years and years ago, as the legal bulwark of the Communist Party."†

With that, McCarthy had not only violated the lawyers' agreement but had ventured into misleading innuendo: Fisher had not continued to be and was not then a National Lawyers Guild member. But the senator, like a bull tormented in the arena, was turning savagely on his adversary in the bow tie.

"I have hesitated to bring that up; but I have been rather bored with your phony requests to Mister Cohn here that he

---

* In his generally sympathetic account, Arthur Herman suggests that McCarthy's drinking may have caused him to "black out" on the Cohn-Welch agreement not to bring up Fisher.

† An obvious reference to the National Lawyers Guild.

personally get every communist out of government before sundown I get the impression that you are quite an actor,* you play for a laugh. I don't think you yourself would ever knowingly aid the communist cause. I think you are unknowingly aiding it when you try to burlesque this hearing . . ."

When McCarthy finished, the Caucus Room was quiet for a moment while Welch composed himself to reply. Slowly, as if to remind McCarthy of all those "point of order" interruptions, he said, "Under the circumstances I must myself have something approaching a personal privilege." He requested McCarthy's attention, and when the latter suggested that he could listen with one ear while talking to someone else, Welch spoke more sharply:

"No, this time, sir, I want you to listen with both ears."

Then, in unhurried, unforgettable words, he added: "Until this moment, Senator, I think I never really gauged your cruelty or your recklessness."

In the same restrained tone, he told how, upon learning of Fisher's NLG membership, he had purposely not asked the younger man to come to Washington:

"Little did I dream you could be so reckless and so cruel as to do an injury to that lad.† It is true he is still with Hale and Dorr. It is true that he will continue to be with Hale and

---

* Some years later Welch did play a role in a James Stewart movie, *Anatomy of a Murder.*

† Fisher was thirty-two years old.

Dorr. It is, I regret to say, equally true that I fear he shall always bear a scar needlessly inflicted by you. If it were in my power to forgive you for your reckless cruelty, I would do so; I like to think I am a gentle man. But your [here a long, effective pause] forgiveness . . . will have to come from someone other than me."

Undaunted as usual, McCarthy tried to counterattack. "Mister Welch talks about this being cruel and reckless. He has been baiting Mister Cohn here for hours. . . . I just give this man's record—"

"Senator, may we not drop this?" Welch cut in. "We know he belonged to the Lawyers Guild. . . . Let us not assassinate this lad further, senator. You have done enough. Have you no sense of decency, sir, at long last? Have you left no sense of decency?"

Even then McCarthy blundered inaccurately on: "Mister Welch talks about any sense of decency. . . . [H]e thinks it is improper for me to give the communist-front record of the man whom he wanted to foist on this committee. But there is no pain in his chest . . . about the attempt to destroy the reputation and take the jobs away from the young men who were working in my committee."

Joseph Welch apparently had had enough:

"Mister McCarthy, I will not discuss this with you any further. You have sat within six feet of me and could have asked me about Fred Fisher. You have seen fit to bring it out and if there is a god in heaven, it will do neither you nor your cause any good. I will *not* discuss it any further. . . . You, Mister Chairman, may, if you will, call the next witness."

Amid the applause that followed, however, McClellan called for adjournment and Mundt brought down the gavel. Welch bowed his head and walked out of the Caucus Room, later weeping in front of the waiting cameras. As Welch left, it apparently dawned on Joe McCarthy that he had somehow gone wrong; rather in bewilderment, he spread his hands and inquired of those around him:

"What did I do?"

BOTH ARTHUR HERMAN and Thomas Doherty have suggested that Welch anticipated McCarthy's breach of the Cohn-Welch agreement and prepared his devastating response in advance. Herman bases his view on an unnamed lawyer's recollection that, after the exchange, he and Welch "walked out of the hearing together, down the hall, around the corner, around another corner, through the corridors of the Senate office building, until finally reporters had quit trailing us and the flash bulbs had quit exploding. Welch looked at me and without changing his expression, the tears still streaming down his face, asked, 'Well, how did it go?'"[61]

This story, however, does not necessarily prove that Welch was merely acting in his responses to McCarthy. It certainly does not disprove Welch's observation that McCarthy needlessly and inaccurately, and therefore recklessly, accused Fisher before a national television audience; or the fact that

Welch himself was falsely charged with having tried to "foist" Fisher on the subcommittee.

Doherty does not mention the anonymous lawyer's account but suggests that Welch's words were too "poetic" and polished to have been extemporaneous.[62] This is a matter of judgment, and Doherty's inference seems to be sheer speculation. His suggestion discounts the cadence, polish, and "poetry" of many other unprepared speeches, on many other occasions—for example, Robert F. Kennedy's memorable remarks to a black audience in Indianapolis on the night of Martin Luther King's murder. Joseph Welch was, long before June 9, 1954, a practiced courtroom lawyer whose forensic skills had often been demonstrated.

Theatrical Welch's words were; and weeping before the cameras was something of a stretch; but that his cutting responses were "prepared in advance," to take advantage of a moment he could not have foreseen, seems highly unlikely.

Prepared or not, Welch's moment of eloquence was the highlight of the hearings—themselves a landmark in television history for their role in bringing down Joe McCarthy. Whether he was seen as a dangerous demagogue or as a national hero, McCarthy like Humpty Dumpty took a great fall; and after those fatal 188 hours in 1954, he never put himself together again.

In January 1954, as Eisenhower began only a second year in the White House, a Gallup Poll had reported that Mc-

Carthy was viewed favorably by 50 percent of the American public. Only 29 percent of respondents felt unfavorable about him, and 21 percent—people who apparently paid little attention to the news—had no opinion. Right after the Army-McCarthy hearings ended that summer, the percentage of those with unfavorable opinions of McCarthy rose 16 points to 45; in a severe drop, only 34 percent still had a favorable impression of him. Again, 21 percent would disclose no opinion. In little more than a month, Joseph N. Welch and Mc-Carthy's own indiscipline—exposed on television for all to see—had stripped McCarthy of his mystique and his power.

Two days after Welch's scornful remarks, one of Mc-Carthy's old enemies, Ralph Flanders of Vermont, walked into the hearing room, made his way among those in attendance, and handed McCarthy a letter. The Wisconsin senator read the message aloud: Flanders was inviting him to be on the Senate floor to hear himself criticized in another Flanders speech.

"Number one," McCarthy said to the audience, in the room and at home, "I will be unable to be present because I am testifying. Number two, I don't have enough interest in any Flanders speech to listen to it. Number three, if you have nothing except the usual smear, gleaned from the smear sheets, then . . . I think you should do it here under oath."

Chairman Mundt railed against "this kind of feuding"; Flanders said he would leave; and McCarthy commented aloud that he would not accuse the elder senator of "vicious-ness but perhaps senility." Later, embellishing the point, he told the press, "I think they should get a net and take him to a good quiet place."[63]

McCarthy's rebuff had been another bad move. When Flanders rose later that day, it was to introduce on the floor Senate Resolution 261, in which Joseph R. McCarthy was de-scribed as "in contempt" of the Senate. If the resolution was approved, McCarthy would have to answer certain questions about his finances, including the old allegation that he had accepted an improper payment from Lustron, a company under the committee's jurisdiction. If he did not or would not answer the questions, the resolution would strip him of the chairmanship of the Government Operations Committee. Flanders's move turned out to be the first step in the Senate's eventual censure of the junior senator from Wisconsin.

Back in the Caucus Room at about the time Flanders was speaking, Roy Cohn—apparently realizing how badly the hearings were going not only for McCarthy but also for him and for his boyfriend G. David Schine—angrily confronted Robert Kennedy. The two young lawyers were bitter enemies from their days working together on the McCarthy staff. A shouting match ensued and Cohn readied a swing at Kennedy; but cameras and cooler heads were present, spectators inter-vened, and no blow was struck.[64]

Six days later the Army-McCarthy hearings were perma-nently adjourned, with melodious obsequies from Everett

Dirksen. ("We have ploughed the long furrow."[65]) In September the subcommittee's unanimous report confirmed what many attentive television viewers, and not a few senators, already had concluded: Roy Cohn, backed and sometimes aided by Senator Joseph R. McCarthy of Wisconsin, had tried repeatedly to browbeat the army into granting special favors to Private G. David Schine. Secretary of the Army Robert Stevens had sought to appease Cohn and McCarthy before finally, under the prodding of President Eisenhower, screwing his courage to the sticking place.

8

★ ★ ★

THIRTY-SIX DAYS of televised hearings had allowed the nation to see Joe McCarthy's browbeating "bad manners" and to grasp his abuse of his office; more importantly, it had been shown on the home screen that he could produce little evidence to support the headlines he had so easily created. The precipitous decline of his favorable Gallup rating dispelled the aura of political power that had protected him. And almost immediately Ralph Flanders's resolution, introduced on June 11, 1954, forced the Senate toward a decision many senators had never wanted to make—thumbs-up or thumbs-down on a controversial colleague with a popular cause.

The Senate would not take such a stand quickly or easily. On June 12 Republican leader William Knowland, a convinced McCarthyite, denounced Flanders for acting "contrary to established procedure in the Senate"[66] by not consulting him before introducing the resolution. Knowland knew an election-year vote on the Flanders motion would divide the slim Republican majority between conservative McCarthyites and moderate Eisenhower Republicans, with Democratic senators then holding the balance of power. Such a vote would also split the general Republican Party along the same fault line. The first Republican administration in twenty years almost inevitably would be damaged. And Knowland could not be sure he could protect his friend or the right-wing anticommunism in which he believed and that had seemed to pay political dividends.

Neither was Minority Leader Lyndon Johnson, despite sometimes intense pressure from liberal senators, yet ready to set the Democrats openly against McCarthy. One reason was that his strongest supporters, the influential southern conservative senators, feared that passage of the Flanders resolution in its original form would threaten the "seniority system" and hence the committee chairmanships on which their power was based. Johnson did not want to risk, moreover, a partisan fight with Democrats pitted against an anticommunist while Republicans defended him; and he did not believe that the votes to carry the Flanders resolution necessarily could be found. The minority leader also faced a Democratic primary in Texas on July 24; and though there was little chance that LBJ would lose his second-term bid to a highly eccentric opponent, Dudley Dougherty, some of Johnson's wealthy backers in Texas were also among Joe McCarthy's major contributors. LBJ had to be careful not to offend them and possibly to follow Lucas and McFarland into the graveyard of Senate Democratic leaders.

On June 15 Knowland succeeded in having Resolution 261 referred to the Committee on Rules, chaired by another fierce McCarthyite, William Jenner of Indiana—thus greatly enhancing the parliamentary difficulties faced by Flanders and his supporters. These supporters were numerous and active, however, particularly among Democrats, and included senators, House members, staff assistants, and outside backers. Several Republican senators, notably John Sherman Cooper of Kentucky and James Duff of Pennsylvania, also aided Flanders; and a crucial financial contributor to the anti-McCarthy effort was Paul Hoffman, a Republican businessman, former Marshall Plan administrator, and strong Eisenhower supporter.

One head count suggested where the matter stood in the beginning: twenty-five Democrats and twelve Republicans *for* the resolution; nineteen Republicans and one Democrat, Pat McCarran of Nevada, *against*. That left thirty-nine of the ninety-six senators either undecided or unwilling to disclose a position—with most unhappy about having to vote at all. A lot of persuasive work remained to be done by those who favored action against Joe McCarthy.[67]

The elderly Flanders showed remarkable backbone. He

was a second-term senator, first elected (as was McCarthy) in 1946, who had already decided to retire in 1958, when he would be seventy-eight years of age. With little to lose, he insisted that he would force a vote before the 1954 session expired; but the Senate Republican policy committee, led by Knowland, believed it had much to lose and voted unanimous opposition to Res. 261. Flanders struck back with a substitute resolution to *censure* the junior senator from Wisconsin rather than deprive him of his chairmanships.

In one stroke the substitute answered southern Democrats' fears that Flanders's resolution would endanger the hallowed seniority system (the substitute "is something I can go along with,"[68] said Walter George of Georgia, the "dean" of southern Democratic senators) and blocked Knowland's power to bury it in the hostile Rules Committee. (A resolution to censure a member was "privileged," in parliamentary terms: it could not be referred to a committee but had to be voted upon directly.) Moreover, a vote to amend or table the new resolution would be as revealing of where senators stood on McCarthy as would be a vote on its substance. Senators would not be able to hide from a decision.

Only three times in history, however, had the Senate censured a member, and none of those instances provided a clear precedent for Flanders's new Resolution 301. By mid-July the pro-resolution count had grown only to forty-two, with twenty senators solidly against it[69] and the rest, for various reasons,

still on the fence. So intense were the pressures* as the November elections approached that even within the Eisenhower
White House moderate Republicans, fearful of party disunity,
appear to have counseled caution.

In cloakrooms and corridors, the *politics* of Res. 301 raged
hotly that summer of 1954. Finally, on the last day of July,
Ralph Flanders—despite ostracism by some of his resentful
party colleagues—proved as good as his word: he called up
his privileged resolution for a vote, spoke briefly in its favor,
and sat down, having forced the Senate at last to face up to
Joe McCarthy.

As THE FLOOR DEBATE on the Flanders resolution began,
Everett Dirksen, sonorous as a pipe organ, denounced Res.
301 as an unfair assault on a fellow senator and a move con-
cocted by left-wingers and communists with whom—Dirksen was sad to say—the honorable senator from Vermont had
naively joined hands. This anticipated attack earned Dirksen
a handshake from McCarthy; but more persuasive was a

---

* Of particular interest today is the announcement by John F. Kennedy of
Massachusetts, with its large Irish Catholic population, that he would vote
for the Flanders resolution only if Minority Leader Johnson did so and a report in the files of the National Committee for an Effective Congress that
Prescott Bush of Connecticut, Eisenhower's golfing companion and grand-
father of George W. Bush, "was favorable but needed encouragement."
Robert Griffith, *The Politics of Fear,* 2nd ed. (Amherst: University of Massachusetts Press, 1987), pp. 286–87.

better-reasoned speech by an undecided Republican, Guy Cordon of Oregon.

Cordon argued that McCarthy—or, in effect, any senator facing censure—deserved both a "bill of particulars" against him and the opportunity to defend himself against such charges before a properly empowered committee. This strong plea for procedural safeguards ignored the fact that McCarthy had already several times defended himself before Senate committees (and made a shambles of most of them)* and that what was at issue in McCarthy's case was not only specific acts but the entire pattern of his behavior since the Wheeling speech in 1950—in short, *McCarthyism* as well as McCarthy.

The Senate, however, was not ready to put McCarthyism on trial. It was hard enough to deal with the man without taking on the *-ism:* who wanted to be vilified for supporting communists? Even Wayne Morse, Cordon's Oregon colleague but certainly not a McCarthyite, supported the demand for particulars and committee referral—the kind of "fair procedure" that Joe McCarthy as chairman and investigator had so often denied *his* targets.† So strong was the effect of

---

* For instance, the panel that had investigated McCarthy's part in the 1950 Maryland election.

† Wayne Morse explained to me years later one of the subtle truths of political—particularly legislative—life: he who controls procedure controls substance.

Cordon's argument that Morse, Fulbright, and even Flanders added a number of "particulars" to Res. 301. Still, there was no clear majority for or against the resolution; still, the 1954 elections were nearing; still, the anti-McCarthy forces urged action that would split the Republican Party.

Under the political pressures of 1954, Bill Knowland—in the parlance of a later time—blinked first: to avoid a show-down vote, he proposed that a select committee of three Republicans and three Democrats consider Flanders's Res. 301. The full Senate would be relieved temporarily of a painful decision and the idea of fair procedure would be served. It was widely believed at the time that the wily Lyndon Johnson* had influenced, perhaps even originated, Knowland's proposal. In the most exhaustive account of Johnson's Senate years, Robert Caro suggests that before Knowland acted, LBJ "had lined up support for the move he wanted, the appointment of . . . a bipartisan select committee . . . by consulting with such key Republicans as Earl Warren and General Jerry Persons, head of the White House congressional liaison team."[70]

At any rate, LBJ and the Democrats leaped to accept the select committee proposal—insisting, however, that the com-

---

* Despite his wary tactics, LBJ had little use for McCarthy and had told his henchman, Bobby Baker: "Joe's just a loud-mouthed drunk . . . the sorriest senator up here. Can't tie his goddam shoes." Morgan, *Reds,* p. 504.

mittee report its decision on the McCarthy matter *before* the Eighty-third Congress adjourned. The much-resisted up-or-down vote was thus assured, even if not before Election Day. Flanders, Fulbright, and other diehards fought for a full and immediate Senate vote; but even they could not have been too disheartened when senators eagerly voted, seventy-five to twelve, for the select committee and delay. Everyone then went home to campaign.

BILL KNOWLAND HAD TAKEN what he apparently considered a strategic gamble. But before the year was out, it seemed to Republicans and Democrats alike, to both pro- and anti-McCarthy senators, that the majority leader had more nearly given away the game. He had nothing like the cunning or strategic sense of Lyndon Johnson, who proceeded—as ample evidence attests—not only to pick the Democratic members of the select committee but to nudge and persuade Knowland into approving what were Johnson's preferences for the Republican members.[71]

The resulting roster consisted entirely of established conservatives (no right-wing McCarthyites but also no liberal Hubert Humphrey or Herbert Lehman to be denounced as a pink or a dupe). On the Democratic side were Edwin C. Johnson of Colorado, one of LBJ's closest friends; John Stennis of Mississippi, a silent power in the Senate; and Sam J. Ervin of North Carolina, a former justice of that state's supreme court. For the Republicans, Knowland (or Johnson) chose Frank Carlson of Kansas, a strong Eisenhower man, and Francis Case of South Dakota, a senator so respectably obscure that only veteran reporters could identify him from the press gallery.

By Senate rules, the chairman had to be a member of Knowland's Republican majority; the two leaders picked Arthur Watkins of Utah, a relatively unknown senator respected in the chamber as a tough Mormon devoted to orderly procedure. The select committee then set rules that left McCarthy little room for the evasive and accusatory tactics of which he had proved himself a master; "we are not unmindful of his genius for disruption," Watkins observed.[72] For example, the Watkins committee ruled that McCarthy and his lawyer, the eminent Edward Bennett Williams of Washington, D.C., could not be recognized at the same time. Williams conceded that McCarthy would remain silent except when testifying, which meant that cross-examination would be left to his lawyer—a major setback for the risible senator.

There was no television, the number of witnesses was strictly limited, and the "particulars"—in effect the charges—were reduced from forty-two to the thirteen least likely to evoke McCarthy's disruptive skills. Among these, significantly, was his "contempt" of a subcommittee that in 1951 and 1952 had heard former Connecticut senator William Benton's resolution to expel him; the Wisconsin senator had adamantly refused to appear before or testify to that panel.

The Watkins hearings began on August 31, 1954. When McCarthy tried his familiar tactic of raising a "point of order" in a public session, Chairman Watkins slapped him down summarily. "The senator is out of order," he declared. "We are not going to be interrupted by these diversions and sidelines."

The committee then adjourned. McCarthy, expecting to proceed as usual, rushed outside to the waiting television cameras. But as he tried to explain how he had just been silenced, he could only sputter:

"I think it's the most unheard of thing I ever heard of."[73]

This ludicrous response suggested how far McCarthy was from his home turf; clearly, these hearings were not going to be anything like the Army-McCarthy exhibition. In fact, after Watkins's display of firmness, McCarthy rarely appeared, leaving his defense to Edward Bennett Williams. But the case against him, when soberly considered absent his hostile presence, was too convincing for even a lawyer as skilled as Ed Williams to shake.

On September 27, after nine public hearings, the hand-picked committee recommended unanimously (an important consideration) that Joseph R. McCarthy should be censured on two counts—first, for his repeated contempt in 1951 and 1952 of the Senate subcommittee* weighing the Benton

---

* Among other offenses, McCarthy had called a subcommittee member, Robert Hendrickson of New Jersey, "a living miracle without brains or guts."

resolution and, second, for his "reprehensible" treatment of General Zwicker. The committee report dealt with the remaining particulars in harsh terms strongly condemnatory of the junior senator from Wisconsin but found none of them warranted censure.

The report provided ample grounds for any senator to vote for censure but said nothing about "McCarthyism" or communists or anticommunists or civil liberties or treason in high places or even defamatory charges—unless the Zwicker case were so construed. McCarthy should be censured, the committee of paragons ruled, for his antagonistic behavior toward other senators and for bringing the Senate into disrepute—*not* for anything he had done or said in public during his anticommunist crusade, however unfair or divisive or derogatory or partisan or insupportable.

No doubt this was the kind of report for which Lyndon Johnson had hoped—one that would certainly bring about a vote against Joe McCarthy. The narrowness of the ground on which the committee demanded censure was no accident. In the summer of 1954, even as the anti-McCarthy debate was progressing from the Senate floor to the Watkins committee, the Congress of the United States—aided and abetted by the Eisenhower administration—was acting on McCarthyism's anticommunist assumptions in the dominant anticommunist climate of American politics. With the Cold War unabated in 1954, both the Senate and the House approved and the president signed

... legislation to strip citizenship from persons convicted of conspiracy to advocate the violent overthrow of government, to make peacetime espionage a capital offense, to require Communist organizations to register all printing equipment, to grant immunity to witnesses before courts, grand juries, and congressional committees in order to compel testimony, to increase the penalties for harboring fugitives and jumping bail, and to broaden and redefine espionage and sabotage laws.[74]

To the so-called Communist Control Act of 1954, Hubert H. Humphrey of Minnesota and other Cold War liberals, backed by Democratic leader Johnson, offered an amendment that civil libertarians believed would violate free speech and tend to deny the right to vote and due process of law.* The amendment was approved, forty-one to thirty-nine, with only one senator, Estes Kefauver of Tennessee, voting against the final amended control act. No one could say, Senate liberals must have thought, that Senate Democrats were left-wing dupes or that they were going to censure Joe McCarthy as a service to the communist conspiracy.

———

* The Humphrey amendment declared the Communist Party an "agency of a hostile foreign power" and therefore not entitled to the rights, privileges, and immunities of other parties.

TOO MANY SENATORS were engaged in tough campaigns—
which might turn on whether they voted for or against Mc-
Carthy (or so it was believed)—for the Senate to vote on the
Watkins report before the November election. Even the
national campaign suggested, however, that the once-lionized
Wisconsin senator had passed from political hero to political
liability. Unlike in 1952, he had few invitations to speak and
played little part in a Republican election effort that continued to emphasize communist subversion but was forcefully
led by Richard Nixon (rather than Dwight Eisenhower).

Whether because of the anticommunist legislation en-
acted by the Eighty-third Congress or despite it, the Democrats fared far better in 1954 than they had in 1952. Most
Democratic incumbents—including Kefauver—were reelected, in some cases against smear campaigns. The Republican liberal Clifford Case was elected in New Jersey, while
Guy Cordon, who had called so eloquently for "fair procedure" for Joe McCarthy, was defeated in Oregon by Democrat Richard Neuberger. Republicans lost eighteen seats in
the House and control of that chamber. Democrats picked
up one Senate seat for a total of forty-eight. If they could
persuade the independent Wayne Morse to vote with them,
Democrats would take control of the Senate and Joe Mc-
Carthy would be out as chairman of the Committee on
Government Operations and hence of his Permanent Investigations Subcommittee.

Lyndon Johnson gave Morse two cherished committee seats—on Foreign Relations and on Banking and Currency. Morse happily switched allegiance, and LBJ, at forty-six, became the youngest Senate majority leader—ultimately one of the most powerful—in American history. Almost the first order of business for him was the long-delayed vote on the Watkins committee report.

McCarthy remained obdurate, refusing all suggestions for compromise, including some from such close colleagues as Dirksen and Styles Bridges. Final debate began on November 29, after McCarthy had entered the hospital for treatment of an elbow injury and been released; the Senate had deferentially adjourned for ten days pending his return. By then, opposition to censure had begun to crystallize, and the once-obscure Francis Case had undermined the unanimity of the Watkins committee on which he had served. First, Case suggested that McCarthy merely apologize; then he openly criticized the report; finally he announced that he would not vote for censure on the Zwicker charge that he had approved with the rest of the Watkins committee. That may have led, on the first day of debate, to the following quiet advice from Lyndon Johnson to the committee chairman:

"Arthur, you are going to have to drop the Zwicker matter. There are at least fifteen Democratic senators who will not vote for the censure resolution if the Zwicker charge is part of it."[75]

That was enough; the Zwicker charge was abandoned,
though McCarthy's documented abuse of the general, and by
inference of the military, was the most lurid of the particulars
the Watkins committee had considered. But McCarthy's
stubborn refusal to yield and his urge to fight back countered
even this limited victory. He entered into the *Congressional
Record* a speech so unacceptably critical of the committee
(the Communist Party "has made a committee of the Senate
its unwilling handmaiden. . . . It did the work of the Communist Party") that Wallace Bennett, Watkins's Utah colleague,
successfully moved for a new charge: abusing the select committee and its chairman.

The debate was bitter and often intemperate, with Jenner
even suggesting that "some members of the Senate might be
secret Communists." John Stennis accused McCarthy of
throwing slime on other senators; and on the TV program
Meet the Press, Sam Ervin suggested that if McCarthy believed what he was saying, he might be suffering from "men-
tal delusion."[76]

On December 2, 1954, cries of "Vote, vote!" filled the
Senate chamber. Finally, the roll was called; its outcome sug-
gested that despite a torrent of outside pressures backing Mc-
Carthy, censure had been all but certain from the start.
Johnson lined up forty-four of his Democrats—John F.
Kennedy not among them—to support the resolution. (Pat
McCarran of Nevada, who would have backed McCarthy,

had died in October.) They were joined by Morse plus twenty-two Republicans (mostly eastern Eisenhower backers) in a resounding sixty-seven to twenty-two vote for censure. Republicans split down the middle, with only old Taft backers staying with Joe McCarthy. The senator himself voted "present," and there were six absentees.

McCarthy made one last show of defiance: apologizing— not to any senator, but to the public for his support of Eisenhower in 1952, when McCarthy claimed to have hoped that the general would be solidly anticommunist. Much of the public and particularly the White House reacted with significant silence; McCarthy was no longer feared and heeded. In January 1955 he faced and survived the ritual gesture of turning over his gavel to the Government Operations Committee's senior Democrat, John McClellan. As if unfazed, McCarthy continued to make harsh speeches on the Senate floor. But they were seldom listened to, sometimes not even attended, in the chamber he once had dominated.

Even worse, the press paid him little attention; those who knew McCarthy believed that the loss of headlines and an entourage of reporters pained him more than the indifference of his colleagues. And a final grab for the front pages resulted only in another fiasco. In June 1955, as Eisenhower prepared to attend a summit conference in Europe, McCarthy introduced a resolution that would have forced the president into a self-defeating confrontation with the Soviet Union over the so-called captive nations of Eastern Europe. Nixon told the president not to take the resolution seriously; he didn't, and the Senate didn't either. Some of McCarthy's closest former allies—Knowland, Hickenlooper, Welker, Dirksen, Mundt—took a forthright stand against his resolution. Only William Jenner, William Langer, and George "Molly" Malone backed him, making up a quartet at the bottom of the Senate pecking order. This last-gasp effrontery was demolished by a vote of seventy-seven to four.

Eisenhower's quip at the time was widely quoted in Washington: "It's no longer McCarthyism. It's McCarthywasm."[77]

AFTER FIRST REMARKING jovially that the censure "wasn't exactly a vote of confidence" and attending that night a rally of thirteen thousand (less than expected) supporters at Madison Square Garden, the usually ebullient McCarthy sank with surprising rapidity from public view and into personal deterioration. He and Jean Kerr McCarthy adopted a five-week-old girl and named her Tierney; the child seemed to bring him at least brief happiness, and the admirably steadfast support of his wife clearly helped him to go on as well as he did.

Still, visitors to their home reported that he gazed emptily at nothing; and his drinking became steady, a scandal and a constant health hazard—by one estimate the senator consumed a bottle a day. Old friends from Wisconsin and his glory days in the Senate were shocked and horrified by the deterioration in mind, body, and presence that they could not help but see.

As the days and weeks trickled by, McCarthy seemed ever more demoralized, sometimes almost dazed, often disheveled, wandering aimlessly about Washington, Capitol Hill, or Wisconsin, enduring a sort of silent treatment from once-deferential senators, checking in and out of the hospital (usually to dry out), ignoring all urgings* that he stop drinking—a stubbly-bearded, foul-breathed shadow of the much-feared inquisitor of 1953 and 1954, a shabby remnant of the man who had tormented two presidents.

It was toward the end of this period, in January 1957, that I encountered and at first failed to recognize McCarthy in the Old Senate Office Building—only thirty months after Joseph N. Welch, in full view of the nation, had flayed him for cruelty and recklessness, a mere two years after his colleagues voted to censure him, and only a few months before his death in May of alcohol-related ailments.

It was in this period, too, early in the congressional session of 1957, that I watched from the Senate press gallery as McCarthy rose to speak, or perhaps to make a motion— nothing of importance. Bill White of the *New York Times*

---

* Including those of doctors, senators, and, repeatedly, Jean Kerr McCarthy, who nevertheless, in later years, always denied that her husband had had a drinking problem.

whispered in my ear: "You watch. Lyndon's going to lay him out like a corpse." And LBJ did. Joe McCarthy—who once had browbeat anyone in his way, insisted on his points of order, and derided his critics—sat down silently, brooding, chastened, slinking off into some darkness of his own. One did not have to know him or even who he was—though this time I did—to perceive that darkness.

When it finally took him only weeks later, on May 2, 1957, a High Requiem Mass was said in the same St. Matthew's Cathedral where McCarthy and Jean Kerr had taken their marriage vows with the Pope's blessing and where, six years later, President Kennedy's funeral service was to take place. An honor guard of U.S. Marines carried McCarthy's emaciated body from the cathedral to Capitol Hill, where seventy of the senators who had helped ruin him attended a service in the Senate chamber.

Then his remains were flown to Wisconsin, where Joe McCarthy was buried in Appleton at the side of his parents, overlooking the Fox River. Almost unnoticed among the graveside mourners was Robert F. Kennedy, who later wrote in his journal that Joe McCarthy was "a very complicated character."[78]

FEW OF THOSE writing about McCarthy have been willing to extend him even that much regard. "Perhaps no other figure in American history has been portrayed so consistently as the essence of evil," concludes Thomas C. Reeves of the University of Wisconsin in his comprehensive biography of McCarthy.

Taking due note of the senator's "native intelligence and . . . formidable energy," Reeves resists the conventional judgment—that Joseph R. McCarthy was a publicity-seeking adventurer who relied on lying and slander and was willing to ruin other people's lives in order to advance his own career. Reeves concedes, however, that McCarthy's positive attributes were "mostly squandered in foolish and damaging causes."[79]

The perception of McCarthy as an unprincipled demagogue* seeking headlines and self-advancement ("a charlatan," Clare Booth Luce called him) is bolstered by the historical fact that, for all his ranting and in all his "investigations," McCarthy never uncovered—much less sent to jail—a single communist, in or out of government. Many of those he pursued later were vindicated in court† or landed on their feet—Assistant Secretary of State William Bundy being an example of the latter.

For all the noise McCarthy made after 1950, he was in fact a latecomer to, and virtually a nonparticipant in, the real anticommunist wars. Richard Nixon had helped expose Alger

---

* Perhaps most forcefully presented by Richard H. Rovere in *Senator Joe McCarthy* (New York: Harcourt Brace Jovanovich, 1959).

† Owen Lattimore, for instance, was acquitted of perjury in 1953, and the Justice Department dropped his case in 1955.

Hiss in 1948; and the major threat of subversion—as well as some notable actual examples—had occurred during the Roosevelt and early Truman wartime and postwar years. This was well before the period of 1950 to 1954, when McCarthy was portraying himself as the scourge of Reds, "pinkos," dupes, and fellow travelers in government.*

Smith Act prosecutions; the antisubversive measures adopted in the Truman and Eisenhower administrations; the testimony of ex-communist witnesses such as Igor Gouzenko, Elizabeth Bentley, and Whittaker Chambers; the decline of the Communist Party USA; even the work of the House Un-American Activities Committee and the Senate Internal Security Committee—however hated by civil libertarians then and since†—had substantially done the job before McCarthy rose to speak in Wheeling.

This makes his undeniable demagoguery even more despicable, because there was no real need or justification for it. It undermines, too, the argument sometimes made that Joe McCarthy must have been "on to something." He was on to

---

* "The timely release of Venona could have shown the American people the true extent of Soviet espionage, which was far-reaching, while showing also that by 1950, when Senator McCarthy got going, it was all but over with. . . . McCarthy was inconsequential to the issue he rode to fame." Morgan, *Reds,* pp. 291–93. But the Venona transcripts were not published until 1995.

† Most of whom, like me, knew little or nothing about the Venona transcripts before their publication in 1995.

nothing but echoes from years gone by, and he tried, fundamentally, to lock the barn after the horse had been stolen.

In his time, moreover, there were real and greater enemies—the Soviet Union with its missiles and military power and the worldwide communist movement. McCarthy did little to preserve U.S. security against these threats, and he actually did great *damage* to his country in its half century of Cold War competition. His assaults on civil liberties; his attacks on the State Department and on Roosevelt-Truman-Eisenhower foreign policies; his insistence that events such as the Korean War resulted from subversion in Washington; his battles against Bohlen, Acheson, Marshall, Truman, and even the Republican Eisenhower*—all undermined what America should have been able to claim as its strength: free and democratic institutions, featuring unfettered dissent.

At Wheeling and in the weeks that followed, McCarthy surely *was* the demagogue that history has considered him. A man who knew how to manipulate Boss Tom Coleman in Wisconsin and who invented for himself a heroic war record could not have been unaware that a Red scare would be politically rewarding to him and his party. Besides, McCarthy was too shrewd, too knowledgeable, too cynical about politics to accept a document such as the Lee List at face value; and

---

* And, of course, the book-burning travels of McCarthy's "junketeering gumshoes" in 1953.

he had to know that his claim to have penetrated State Department security to obtain the list's dossiers was false.

That was in 1950, and it is impossible to believe that for most of the years that followed—before his censure—McCarthy did not realize he had tapped into a rich political vein and was not determined to exploit it for his own good and that of the party that egged him on. If he did not entirely believe in the anticommunist threat he denounced or in the perfidy of all his opponents, he clearly loved the excitement, the aura of political power, the regard of colleagues, and perhaps, above all, the headlines that resulted from his every statement, his wildest charges, his most daring battles. He relished the notoriety he achieved, the risks involved in the career he made, the real or imagined challenges to his position, the phrases he made and repeated, the foes he vanquished, the critics he rebutted—and always the brawling, bloody alley fights in which he envisioned himself engaged and usually triumphant.

Just prior to the censure vote, Everett Dirksen visited McCarthy in the hospital and brought him a conciliatory letter to sign, along with a bottle of whiskey. McCarthy was unmoved and refused the letter, though not the whiskey.

"I don't crawl," he told Dirksen. "I learned to fight in an alley. That's all I know."[80]

This was his true faith: in fighting, whomever the opponent, whatever the odds. And if in the combat some people or even the nation were damaged (in the struggle against cancer "some healthy tissue on the fringe will be destroyed"), still, so keen an observer as Alexander Hamilton once remarked, "demagogues are not always inconsiderable persons."[81] In his far different context, nearly two centuries later, Joe McCarthy was anything but inconsiderable.

Undaunted by persistent failure, he displayed a relentless if sometimes misplaced will to continue the struggle—the sort of doggedness that carried him through Little Wolf High School in one year. His flair for drama and phrasemaking outpaced his Red-hunting competitors (no dictionary today refers to "Dirksenism" or even "Nixonism"); he seemed to know instinctively, as with that long-ago campaign pamphlet in Wisconsin, that *The Newspapers Say . . .* was a more enticing title than *McCarthy for Senator.* Judge Werner certainly could have testified that Joe McCarthy was not afraid to take on anyone; and he consistently did—even a president of his own party. If the battle was risky, McCarthy made risk taking seem patriotic, the act of a man so convinced of his cause that he was reckless of his own safety.

He played the press as if it were his personal chessboard. He knew how to create news and headlines, how to top an opponent's story, how to feed a press hungry for sensation and enamored of those who provided it. A phenomenal political juggler, McCarthy usually managed to keep all balls in the air—but when he did misjudge, he was dexterous enough to recover and go on with the act.

Knowing little of history or philosophy, McCarthy's innate sense of what the American people feel and believe—and want to hear—may yet classify him as a master politician. A dangerous man to corner, as William Benton and others learned, McCarthy was skilled and unscrupulous at fighting back. It was this biting-and-gouging approach to life and battle, not abandoned even as censure impended, that finally crushed him—not his demagoguery, much less the excesses of McCarthyism, but a fight he could not win and would not avoid.

AMPLE, IF PERHAPS BIASED, testimony from many who knew and followed him contends that McCarthy ultimately became a sincere warrior in what he believed was a patriotic cause; Jean Kerr McCarthy always maintained that he was a true believer (as she was).

Some events seem to support this heretical view. Would even a risk taker have chanced an unnecessary attack on an icon such as George Marshall? The acceptance that McCarthy found on his side of the Senate and in public esteem after Wheeling could hardly have failed to gratify a man who so craved approval and had been so deprived of it—and may have convinced McCarthy that he was on the right track. The opposition he aroused from Democrats, liberals, leftists, and Senate traditionalists probably signaled the same point: that Joe McCarthy was boldly challenging the hidden influences taking the nation down the wrong road.

McCarthy's attorney, Edward Bennett Williams, believed with Dirksen that had McCarthy apologized for his Senate behavior, *not* for his anticommunist campaign, he might have defeated the censure motion—Lyndon Johnson, in that hypothesis, not being able to hold the southern conservatives in line. Surely a cynic would have apologized with tongue in cheek, all the while chuckling inside at the gullibility of his opponents.

McCarthy didn't compromise, however, and he did attack Marshall gratuitously. It seems to me idle to argue that he was *not* a demagogue, but it is insufficient to dismiss him as *only* a demagogue. If he enjoyed his success, he was not entirely sanguine about its cost in ruined lives and damaged careers. McCarthy *was* "a very complicated character," and in Robert Kennedy's further judgment:

> [McCarthy] would get a guilty feeling and get hurt after he blasted somebody. . . . He was sensitive and yet insensitive. He didn't anticipate the results of what he was doing. He was very thoughtful of his friends and yet he could be so cruel to others.[82]

Joseph R. McCarthy was a demagogue, certainly, but— so far from being inconsiderable—he also was intelligent, energetic, audacious, personally generous, and gifted with dramatic flair and sometimes a brusque sort of charm. Too avidly craving the affirmation of others, too recklessly seeking it in the battle he exalted, McCarthy too carelessly believed that the approval he won justified the means of its achievement. A half century after his death, it is easy to revile him but harder to see him as a victim of human aspiration, who fought desperately and with uncommon success to achieve the wrong dream.

Notes

CHAPTER ONE

1. Thomas C. Reeves, *The Life and Times of Joe McCarthy: A Biography* (Lanham, MD: Madison Books, 1997), p. 102.
2. Robert Griffith, *The Politics of Fear: Joseph R. McCarthy and the Senate,* 2nd ed. (Amherst: University of Massachusetts Press, 1987), p. 50.
3. Reeves, *Life and Times,* p. 224.
4. Robert Donovan, *Conflict and Crisis: The Presidency of Harry S. Truman, 1945–1948* (New York: Norton, 1977), p. 211.

CHAPTER TWO

5. This account of Joseph R. McCarthy's career before he entered the U.S. Senate in early 1947 is derived from the far more detailed record in Reeves, *Life and Times.*
6. Ibid., p. 24.
7. Conrad Black, *Franklin Delano Roosevelt: Champion of Freedom* (New York: Public Affairs, 2003), p. 405.
8. Ted Morgan, *Reds: McCarthyism in Twentieth-Century America* (New York: Random House, 2001), p. 328.
9. Reeves, *Life and Times,* p. 30.
10. Ibid., p. 46.

CHAPTER THREE

11. Reeves, *Life and Times,* p. 76.

12. Arthur Krock, *Memoirs: Sixty Years on the Firing Line* (New York: Funk & Wagnalls, 1968), p. 343.

13. This description of McCarthy's early years in the Senate relies heavily on the far more detailed account in Griffith, *Politics of Fear.*

14. Morgan, *Reds,* pp. 362, 368.

15. Griffith, *Politics of Fear,* p. 56.

16. Ibid., p. 57.

17. The names of Lattimore and Jessup, like those of Shapley and Schuman, do not appear even in the index to the most authoritative account of the Venona Project. John Earl Hynes and Harvey Klehr, *Venona: Decoding Soviet Espionage in America* (New Haven, CT: Yale University Press, 1999).

18. Griffith, *Politics of Fear,* p. 77.

19. Ibid., p. 75.

CHAPTER FOUR

20. Morgan, *Reds,* pp. 374–76. These pages include the "more than 40" and "awash in treachery" quotations.

21. Ibid., pp. 82, 85.

22. Griffith, *Politics of Fear,* p. 96.

23. For a fully detailed account of the Tydings-Butler contest, see U.S. Congress, Senate, 82d Congress, First Session, Committee on Rules and Administration, *Maryland Senatorial Election of 1950.*

24. Alonzo Hamby, *Man of the People: A Life of Harry S. Truman* (New York: Oxford University Press, 1995), p. 564.

25. Griffith, *Politics of Fear,* p. 159.

CHAPTER FIVE

26. David M. Oshinsky, *A Conspiracy So Immense: The World of Joe McCarthy* (New York: Free Press, 1983), pp. 194–95.

27. Reeves, *Life and Times,* p. 437.

28. William B. Ewald Jr., *Eisenhower the President: Crucial Days, 1951–1960* (Englewood Cliffs, NJ: Prentice-Hall, 1981), p. 60.

29. Reeves, *Life and Times,* p. 438.

30. *Wisconsin State Journal* (Madison), October 3, 1952; *St. Louis Post-Dispatch,* October 4, 1952.
31. Ewald, *Eisenhower,* pp. 60–61; William H. Lawrence, *Six Presidents, Too Many Wars* (New York: Saturday Review Press, 1972), pp. 194–97.
32. Reeves, *Life and Times,* pp. 439–40.
33. This account of McCarthy and McCarthyism in the 1952 campaign relies heavily on longer and more detailed passages in ibid., pp. 440–53.
34. Robert A. Caro, *Master of the Senate: The Years of Lyndon Johnson* (New York: Knopf, 2002), p. 547.

CHAPTER SIX
35. Athan Theoharis, *Chasing Spies: How the FBI Failed in Counter-Intelligence but Promoted the Politics of McCarthyism in the Cold War Years* (Chicago: Ivan R. Dee, 2002), pp. 205–7; Caro, *Master of the Senate,* pp. 548–49; Morgan, *Reds,* pp. 449–50.
36. Reeves, *Life and Times,* p. 406; Caro, *Master of the Senate,* p. 548.
37. Theoharis, *Chasing Spies,* pp. 198–209.
38. *Journal of Blacks in Higher Education* (Summer 2004): 38–40.
39. *New York Times,* May 6, 2003, p. A20, after publication of the transcripts of closed subcommittee hearings held in 1953 and 1954.
40. Ibid.
41. Robert F. Kennedy, *The Enemy Within: The McClellan Committee's Crusade Against Jimmy Hoffa and Corrupt Labor Unions* (New York: Popular Library Reprint, 1960).
42. Morgan, *Reds,* p. 444.
43. Ibid., p. 445.
44. Tom Wicker, *Dwight D. Eisenhower, 1953–1961* (New York: Times Books, 2002), pp. 58–59; Morgan, *Reds,* pp. 446–47.
45. Morgan, *Reds,* p. 455.
46. Robert H. Ferrell, ed., *The Diary of James C. Hagerty: Eisenhower in Mid-Course, 1954–1955* (Bloomington: Indiana University Press, 1983), p. 43.
47. Morgan, *Reds,* pp. 478–84.
48. Ibid., p. 468.

49. Ibid., p. 474; Lawrence, *Six Presidents,* p. 199.
50. Wicker, *Eisenhower,* pp. 56–65.
51. Morgan, *Reds,* p. 476.
52. Caro, *Master of the Senate,* quoting LBJ's brother, Sam Houston Johnson, p. 552.

CHAPTER SEVEN
53. Thomas Doherty, *Cold War, Cool Medium: Television, McCarthyism, and American Culture* (New York: Columbia University Press, 2003). The cost figures are at p. 201, the Hennings remark at p. 210.
54. Morgan, *Reds,* p. 486.
55. Arthur Herman, *Joseph McCarthy: Reexamining the Life and Legacy of America's Most Hated Senator* (New York: Free Press, 2000), p. 262.
56. Morgan, *Reds,* p. 490; Doherty, *Cold War,* p. 229.
57. Steven Ambrose, *Eisenhower, Soldier and President* (New York: Simon & Schuster, 1990), p. 365; Ferrell, *Hagerty,* p. 53.
58. Raoul Berger, *Executive Privilege: A Constitutional Myth* (Cambridge, MA: Harvard University Press, 1974), p. 266.
59. Herman, *Joseph McCarthy,* p. 269.
60. Roy M. Cohn, *McCarthy* (New York: New American Library, 1968), pp. 202–3.
61. This quotation is from a footnote, not the author's full text, in Griffith, *Politics of Fear,* p. 260n.
62. Doherty, *Cold War,* pp. 208–9.
63. Morgan, *Reds,* p. 497.
64. Ibid., p. 498.
65. Ibid., p. 498.

CHAPTER EIGHT
66. Griffith, *Politics of Fear,* p. 277.
67. Ibid., p. 283.
68. Morgan, *Reds,* p. 499.
69. Griffith, *Politics of Fear,* p. 285.
70. Caro, *Master of the Senate,* p. 554.

71. See ibid. for a graphic account of this process as recalled by William S. White of the *New York Times*.
72. Morgan, *Reds*, p. 501.
73. Griffith, *Politics of Fear*, p. 299.
74. Ibid., p. 292.
75. Morgan, *Reds*, p. 503.
76. Ibid., pp. 502–3.
77. Ibid., p. 505.
78. Arthur M. Schlesinger Jr., *Robert Kennedy and His Times* (Boston: Houghton Mifflin, 1978), p. 173.
79. Reeves, *Life and Times*, p. 675.
80. Oshinsky, *Conspiracy*, p. 488.
81. During the constitutional debates of 1789. Ron Chernow, *Alexander Hamilton* (New York: Penguin, 2004), p. 233.
82. Herman, *Joseph McCarthy*, p. 306, quoting Robert Kennedy's personal journal.

Index